The WEALTHY Soul:

Ignite Your Passion, Work Less, Earn More

By Ruby Allure

For all those wonderful souls who feel ready to ignite their passions and share them with the world!

CHAPTER 1	6
FOREWORD	6
CHAPTER 2	9
INTRODUCTION:	9
THE WEALTHY SOUL - IGNITE YOUR PASSION, WORK LESS, EARN MORE	9
PART 1:	14
IGNITE YOUR PASSION	14
CHAPTER 3	15
DISCOVERING YOUR PASSIONS	15
CHAPTER 4	22
ALIGNING PASSION WITH PURPOSE	22
CHAPTER 5	33
OVERCOMING OBSTACLES	33
PART 2	43
WEALTH AS WONDER	43
CHAPTER 6	45
RETHINKING WEALTH	45
CHAPTER 7	58
CULTIVATING GRATITUDE	58
EMBRACING GRATITUDE AS A TRANSFORMATIVE PRACTICE	58
CHAPTER 8	68
EMBRACING ABUNDANCE MENTALITY:	68
CULTIVATING A MIND-SET OF ABUNDANCE	68
PART 3	75
CONTRIBUTING AND CONTENT	75
CHAPTER 9	77
THE POWER OF CONTRIBUTION	77
CHAPTER 10	85

FINDING PURPOSE IN SERVICE	85
CHAPTER 11	95
NURTURING RELATIONSHIPS	95
PART 4	102
PURPOSE WITH PEACE	102
CHAPTER 12	104
CLARIFYING YOUR PURPOSE	104
CHAPTER 13	111
BALANCING AMBITION AND INNER PEACE	111
CHAPTER 14	117
MINDFULNESS AND SELF-CARE	117
PART 5	127
TIME AND TRANQUILLITY	127
CHAPTER 15	128
TIME AND TRANQUILLITY	128
CHAPTER 16	138
PRIORITISING SELF-CARE AND LEISURE	138
CHAPTER 17	144
CREATING BOUNDARIES	144
PART 6	150
MONEY MASTERY & MANIFESTING	150
CHAPTER 18	152
MONEY MINDSET SHIFTS	152
CHAPTER 19	159
ABUNDANCE CONSCIOUSNESS	159
CHAPTER 20	164
SMART MONEY HABITS	164
PART 7	169
INFECTIOUS FINANCIAL ENTHUSIASM	169

CHAPTER 21 171
INSPIRING OTHERS 171
CHAPTER 22 179
LEADING BY EXAMPLE 179
CHAPTER 24 188
SPREADING FINANCIAL LITERACY 188
CHAPTER 25 198
IGNITION… 198

CHAPTER 1
FOREWORD

There is a common misconception that spiritual people can't be wealthy. What a clever saboteur to stop people igniting into their full potential. This restrictive belief and concept made me wonder how a soul can reach its true potential, contribute to the world, and have a beautiful abundant financial by-product.

My observation is that power and wealth hold hands. Financial abundance enables choice. Money anxieties shrink the brain and keep an individual caught up in a survival mode. While that poor soul is simply surviving how can they ignite, illuminate, and inspire?

The truth is we need to pay bills if we are to remain within our current system. Soooo with all of that in mind, I received a 'whisper' which directed me to write this book. I also had a wonderful epiphany... the by-product of aligned contribution can be financial abundance. That financial abundance can be used to do good. For me that good is in the form of planting trees. When your financial goblet overflows then the excess can be used for a greater good - isn't that enough of a spiritual motivation in itself?

In the realm where spirits soar,
A truth untold, we shall explore,
It's okay to be both spirit and wealth,
Ignite your passions, embrace your true self.

For too long, a belief held tight,
That spiritual souls must shun the light,
That earthly riches and sacred fire,

Could never merge, nor inspire.

But hear me now, dear soul divine,
A revelation to truly shine,
Your purpose, your flame, an inner guide,
Can lead to riches, far and wide.

In the depths of your ignited core,
Lies a purpose, an ever-growing lore,
Let it guide you, let it unfold,
As you set forth, a story untold.

For as you walk upon this Earth,
Embrace your light, give it birth,
Unleash your passions, let them roam,
For they shall lead you to your home.

With every step, you'll start to see,
Wealth and abundance, a symphony,
Not as goals, but as by-products rare,
Of a soul awakened, beyond compare.

Embrace your purpose, let it soar,
A beacon of light, forevermore,
For when you align with what is true,
The world will bask in the light of you.

Let love be your currency, joy your creed,
And watch as miracles take seed,
The universe shall conspire and conspire,
To manifest dreams that will never tire.

So, fear not, dear spirit, as you rise,
Your spiritual journey, your worldly ties,
Embrace the truth, let it unfold,
That it's okay to be spirit and gold.

May your passions ignite, and purpose ignite,
As you shine your light with all your might,
For in the union of spirit and wealth,
You create a world of joy and health.

R.A

CHAPTER 2
INTRODUCTION:
THE WEALTHY SOUL - IGNITE YOUR PASSION, WORK LESS, EARN MORE

In a world where the pursuit of success often seems synonymous with tireless work, excessive hours, and sacrificing personal fulfilment, there exists a belief, both perplexing and pervasive, that spiritual individuals must resign themselves to a life of meagre means. Yet, nothing could be further from the truth.

Welcome to "The Wealthy Soul: Ignite Your Passion, Work Less, Earn More." In this transformative journey, we shatter the myth that spirituality and material abundance are incompatible. We invite you to embark on a remarkable exploration that challenges conventional wisdom and opens new pathways towards prosperity while nurturing the depths of your soul.

At the core of this book lies the conviction that passion is the key to unlocking unparalleled success and abundance. It is an unwavering belief that your spiritual inclinations need not restrain your financial aspirations. Instead, we will unveil the powerful synergy that emerges when you align your deepest desires with your professional pursuits.

Drawing upon the wisdom of ancient philosophies, modern success principles, and real-life stories of individuals who have redefined their relationship with work and wealth, "The Wealthy Soul" serves as your guide on this extraordinary quest. It illuminates the path to building a thriving career while honouring your spiritual essence, enriching your soul, and creating a life of true abundance.

In the chapters that follow, we will delve into practical strategies, mindset shifts, and actionable steps that enable you to work less and earn more. We will explore the notion that by embracing your passions, igniting your soul, and tapping into your unique gifts, you have the power to cultivate a remarkable existence—one that blends material prosperity with deep spiritual fulfilment.

This book is not a mere blueprint for financial success but an invitation to embrace a holistic approach to life—a philosophy that recognises the interconnectedness of your inner well-being and external manifestations of wealth. It empowers you to transcend limitations, release self-imposed barriers, and embody a mindset of abundance in every aspect of your existence.

"The Wealthy Soul" is a beacon of hope for those who yearn to break free from the shackles of limiting beliefs. It is a manifesto for individuals who refuse to accept the false dichotomy between spiritual enrichment and financial prosperity. By embarking on this transformative journey, you will uncover the extraordinary truth that your spiritual essence can be the catalyst for unlimited abundance in all aspects of your life.

So, dear reader, are you ready to ignite your passion, work less, and earn more? Let us embark together on this enlightening path, where spirituality and prosperity intertwine, and where your wealth and soul find harmony in an extraordinary dance of fulfilment and abundance.

The process of becoming a wealthy soul will be divided into meaningful parts:

Part 1: Ignite Your Passion

- Discovering Your Passions: Unveiling the core desires that fuel your soul and bring you joy.
- Aligning Passion with Purpose: Understanding how to channel your passions into meaningful work that aligns with your values and contributes to your overall fulfilment.
- Overcoming Obstacles: Identifying and overcoming obstacles that may hinder the pursuit of your passions and finding the resilience to persist in the face of challenges.

Part 2: Wealth as Wonder

- Rethinking Wealth: Shifting your mindset and expanding your definition of wealth to encompass more than just material possessions.
- Cultivating Gratitude: Embracing gratitude as a transformative practice that fosters abundance and opens the doors to greater opportunities.
- Embracing Abundance Mentality: Cultivating a mindset of abundance and recognising that there is enough for everyone, dispelling scarcity thinking.

Part 3: Contributing and Content

- The Power of Contribution: Discovering the joy and fulfilment that comes from making a positive impact on others and the world around you.
- Finding Purpose in Service: Exploring how aligning your work with a greater purpose can lead to deep contentment and a sense of fulfilment.
- Nurturing Relationships: Recognising the importance of building authentic connections and fostering meaningful relationships that contribute to your overall well-being.

Part 4: Purpose with Peace

- Clarifying Your Purpose: Reflecting on your life's purpose and finding clarity on how it intersects with your professional endeavours.
- Balancing Ambition and Inner Peace: Cultivating inner peace and harmony while pursuing your goals, creating a balanced and sustainable approach to success.
- Mindfulness and Self-Care: Embracing practices of mindfulness, self-care, and self-compassion to nurture your well-being and maintain a sense of peace throughout your journey.

Part 5: Time and Tranquillity

- Time Management Strategies: Exploring effective time management techniques that allow you to work less, optimise productivity, and create more time for the things that matter most to you.

- Prioritising Self-Care and Leisure: Recognising the importance of rest, leisure, and self-care in maintaining a healthy work-life balance and sustaining long-term success.
- Creating Boundaries: Establishing boundaries to protect your time, energy, and overall well-being, enabling you to focus on what truly matters.

Part 6: Money Manifesting

- Money Mind-set Shifts: Identifying and transforming limiting beliefs and negative associations surrounding money, empowering you to manifest greater financial abundance.
- Embracing Abundance Consciousness: Cultivating a mindset of abundance and attracting wealth through positive thoughts, intentions, and actions.
- Smart Money Habits: Exploring practical financial strategies, including budgeting, investing, and creating multiple streams of income, to build and sustain wealth.

Part 7: Infectious Financial Enthusiasm

- Inspiring Others: Sharing your financial journey, successes, and lessons with others, inspiring and empowering them to embrace their own path to wealth and fulfilment.
- Leading by Example: Becoming a beacon of financial enthusiasm and demonstrating how aligning passion, purpose, and prosperity can create a ripple effect of positive change.
- Spreading Financial Literacy: Advocating for financial education and equipping others with the tools and knowledge to make informed financial decisions.

PART 1:

IGNITE YOUR PASSION

Part 1: Ignite Your Passion

Welcome, adventurer of the soul, to the extraordinary quest of self-discovery! Prepare to embark on a whimsical journey, where we shall uncover the treasures hidden within the depths of your being. Beyond the realm of everyday obligations and societal expectations, lies a landscape brimming with vibrant passions and untamed desires. Are you ready to delve into the enchanted realms of your true essence? Let us venture forth and unveil the mysteries that await!

Through Part 1: Ignite Your Passion, you'll embark on a transformative journey of self-discovery, purpose alignment, and resilience-building. By the end of this section, you'll have a profound understanding of your passions, their connection to your purpose, and the tools to overcome obstacles along the way. Get ready to ignite the fire within and embark on a path of fulfilment and joy as you embrace and unleash your passions upon the world.

CHAPTER 3
DISCOVERING YOUR PASSIONS

In this chapter, we embark on a journey of self-discovery to unveil the core desires that fuel your soul and bring you unparalleled joy. Through introspection, reflection, and exploration, we will uncover the passions that lie dormant within you, waiting to be ignited. We'll delve into exercises and techniques to help you connect with your true essence and identify the activities that make your heart sing.

A fun example: Once upon a time, in a quaint little town nestled amidst rolling hills, lived a woman named Clara. She was known by her neighbours as a kind-hearted and content soul, but Clara often felt like there was something missing in her life. One sunny morning, as she sipped her tea and gazed out the window, a spark of curiosity ignited within her.

Feeling an urge to explore, Clara decided to embark on a journey of self-discovery. She packed a small bag, donned her favourite hat, and set off on an adventure to uncover the unexpected passions that lay dormant within her.

Her first stop was a bustling pottery studio in a nearby village. As she stepped inside, Clara was immediately captivated by the sight of clay spinning on the pottery wheel. Curiosity tugged at her, and she approached the potter, asking if she could give it a try. With skilled guidance, Clara's hands molded the clay into shapes she never thought possible. As she sculpted, she felt a sense of peace and fulfilment wash over her. It was in that moment, covered in clay and with a wide smile on her face, that Clara discovered her hidden passion for pottery.

Eager to uncover more, Clara journeyed to a bustling city where she stumbled upon a street performer playing a lively tune on the accordion. Mesmerised by the music, she found herself tapping her feet and swaying to the rhythm. The performer noticed Clara's enthusiasm and invited her to join in. Clara hesitated at first, feeling self-conscious, but as she embraced the accordion, a wave of joy washed over her. The unexpected passion for music surged through her veins, and she realised that she had a talent for creating melodies that touched the hearts of others.

Continuing her adventure, Clara found herself in a tranquil forest clearing, where she encountered a group of hikers practicing yoga. Drawn to their serenity and grace, she decided to join them in a gentle flow. As she moved through the poses, Clara felt an incredible sense of grounding and connection to her body. With each breath, she discovered her passion for yoga—a path that not only nurtured her own well-being but also held the potential to guide others towards balance and inner peace.

Throughout her journey, Clara stumbled upon unexpected passions that filled her days with joy, purpose, and connection. Pottery, music, and yoga became her guides, shaping her newfound path of self-expression and fulfilment.

As Clara returned home, her heart brimming with excitement, she shared her journey and passions with her friends and neighbours. They marvelled at her transformation and were inspired to embark on their own quests of self-discovery. Clara's unexpected passions ignited a spark within her community, setting off a ripple effect of curiosity, exploration, and fulfilment.

From that day forward, Clara's life was never the same. She embraced her unexpected passions with enthusiasm, spreading joy and creativity wherever she went. And in doing so, she not only discovered the treasures within herself but also inspired others to embark on their own journeys of self-discovery, knowing that the most extraordinary passions often lie in the most unexpected places.

Dance of the Heart:

Embrace the rhythm of your soul and let your body become a vessel of expression. Set aside a dedicated space, put on some uplifting music, and let yourself be guided by the melodies. Allow your body to move freely, unencumbered by self-judgment or restraint. Notice the sensations, the emotions that arise as you dance. Pay attention to the moments when your heart leaps with joy when time seems to disappear. Capture those fleeting glimpses of pure passion and let them guide you towards the activities that truly ignite your soul.

Nature's Whispers:

Step into the embrace of nature's wisdom and let it guide you to your passions. Find a peaceful outdoor setting—a lush forest, a serene beach, or even a blooming garden. As you immerse yourself in the natural surroundings, open your senses and become fully present. Observe the sights, smells, sounds, and textures of the environment. Let nature speak to you, whispering its secrets and calling forth your passions. Notice what draws your attention, what sparks curiosity, and what fills you with a sense of wonder. These subtle clues from nature can lead you towards the passions waiting to be discovered.

Time Capsule of Joy:

Take a nostalgic journey back in time to reconnect with the activities that brought you pure joy as a child. Set aside a quiet moment and recall the innocent pleasures that made your heart soar. Did you love painting, playing an instrument, or exploring the mysteries of the universe? Write down a list of these cherished childhood passions and select one to reignite. Dive back into that activity, allowing yourself to experience the joy and wonder as if you were that carefree child once again. Pay attention to the feelings that arise within you and let them guide you towards passions that have stood the test of time.

Once upon a time, in a charming neighbourhood filled with laughter and nostalgia, lived a woman named Emily. One sunny afternoon, while cleaning out her attic, she stumbled upon a dusty, forgotten box tucked away in the corner. Curiosity piqued, she blew off the cobwebs and opened it, revealing a treasure trove of childhood mementos.

Among the trinkets and treasures, Emily discovered a worn-out diary filled with entries from her younger self. With a mischievous grin, she settled into a cosy chair, ready to take a journey back in time—a journey of pure joy.

As she flipped through the diary's pages, memories came flooding back like a tidal wave of happiness. Emily's heart swelled with nostalgia as she recalled the innocent pleasures of her youth. She remembered the carefree afternoons spent pedalling her beloved bicycle down the neighbourhood streets, her pigtails bouncing with each joyful leap over imaginary ramps.

Inspired by her childhood adventures, Emily hatched a mischievous plan. She dusted off her bicycle, now a tad rusted and forgotten, and with a youthful twinkle in her eye, she decided to relive those whimsical moments of joy. She set off on her two-wheeled time machine, with the wind ruffling her hair and a mischievous grin on her face.

Emily pedalled through the neighbourhood, her laughter blending with the sound of the wind in her ears. She leaped over imaginary ramps once more, her bicycle soaring through the air, as if she could defy gravity itself. The familiar streets transformed into a playground of boundless delight, evoking memories of childhood friendships and the thrill of endless summer days.

As she rode, she attracted the attention of her neighbours, who peered out their windows, their curiosity piqued by this grown woman relishing in childlike bliss. They couldn't help but smile at the sight of Emily's carefree spirit, her contagious laughter filling the air.

Children joined in the joyful escapade, their own bicycles bouncing alongside Emily's. The once-silent streets now echoed with the exuberance of youthful delight. They created a whimsical procession, with Emily at the helm, leading a band of adventurers back to the timeless realm of unadulterated joy.

With each pedal and playful leap, Emily and her newfound companions tapped into a forgotten wellspring of pure happiness. They were reminded that the simple pleasures of childhood hold a timeless magic—a magic that can be rekindled with a dash of courage and a sprinkle of nostalgia.

And so, on that sunny day, in a neighbourhood filled with laughter and wonder, Emily and her fellow adventurers embraced the Time Capsule of Joy, cycling through the streets, hearts brimming with childlike glee. They reminded the world that the key to everlasting joy lies not only in the past but also within our hearts, waiting to be rediscovered, rekindled, and shared with others.

And as the sun began to set, casting a golden glow upon their playful escapade, they returned to their homes with hearts full and spirits alight, forever cherishing the rediscovered treasures of their childhood, forever knowing that joy knows no age, and forever ready to embark on new adventures, one pedal at a time.

Through these unconventional exercises, you will embark on a delightful quest of self-discovery. Let the dance, nature's whispers, and childhood joys be your guides as you unravel the passions that lie within you. Embrace the journey with an open heart and a playful spirit, for within these exercises lie the keys to unlocking the treasures that bring you unparalleled joy. Now, let the adventure begin!

CHAPTER 4
ALIGNING PASSION WITH PURPOSE

Welcome, intrepid seeker, to the transformative realm where passion intertwines with purpose, and dreams take flight on the wings of meaning. In this chapter, we embark on a profound exploration of aligning your passions with a greater purpose—a journey that will illuminate the path to a life of profound fulfilment and resonant impact. Prepare to dive deep into the depths of your being as we uncover the intricate threads that weave your passions and purpose together.

Once your passions are unveiled, we delve deeper into the profound connection between passion and purpose. We explore how aligning your passions with a greater purpose brings a sense of meaning and fulfilment to your life. We'll guide you through a process of introspection and visioning to help you identify how your passions can be channelled into meaningful work that aligns with your values, beliefs, and overarching life purpose.

1. The Puzzle of Purpose:

Gather a collection of puzzle pieces, each representing a different aspect of your passions, skills, and values. Spread them out before you like a colourful mosaic of possibilities. As you examine each piece, reflect on how it aligns with your deepest values and beliefs. Then, with playful curiosity, begin piecing them together, creating a visual representation of your purpose. Let the puzzle guide you towards a greater understanding of how your unique qualities fit together to serve a meaningful purpose in the world.

Once upon a time, in a bustling city full of dreamers and seekers, there lived a man named Benjamin. He was a man of many talents and passions, yet he felt adrift in a sea of possibilities, unsure of how to weave them together into a purposeful life. One day, as Benjamin found himself surrounded by the chaos of everyday life, a peculiar idea whispered in his ear—an idea that would forever change the course of his journey.

Benjamin decided to gather a collection of puzzle pieces, each representing a different aspect of his passions, skills, and values. He carefully selected pieces that symbolised his love for music, his desire to create art, his knack for problem-solving, and his deep-rooted belief in the power of compassion. With anticipation in his heart, he spread the pieces out before him like a colourful mosaic of possibilities.

As Benjamin examined each piece, he allowed his mind to wander and reflect on how they aligned with his deepest values and beliefs. With each puzzle piece, he felt a spark of recognition, a glimmer of connection to his core. Excitement bubbled within him as he realised the profound significance of each fragment of his being.

With playful curiosity and a heart brimming with hope, Benjamin began piecing the fragments together. He marvelled at how the notes of a melody intertwined with the strokes of a paintbrush, how his problem-solving skills merged seamlessly with his compassion for others. Gradually, a visual representation of his purpose emerged—an intricate puzzle taking shape before his eyes.

As Benjamin continued to explore the puzzle, he discovered the threads that connected each piece, weaving a tapestry of meaning and possibility. He saw how his passion for music could be channelled into creating healing experiences for others, how his artistic abilities could be used to ignite emotions and inspire change, and how his problem-solving skills could be employed to address societal challenges with empathy and innovation.

Guided by the puzzle, Benjamin gained a greater understanding of how his unique qualities fit together to serve a meaningful purpose in the world. With newfound clarity and purpose, he embarked on a remarkable journey, using his gifts and passions to make a difference in the lives of others. He composed melodies that stirred souls, painted vibrant murals that transformed communities, and spearheaded projects that brought positive change to those in need.

As Benjamin embraced his purpose, his impact radiated far and wide. People were inspired by his ability to weave his passions into a cohesive tapestry of service and creativity. His story became a beacon of hope for others who were seeking to align their own passions and values. Benjamin's puzzle had not only guided him towards a life of purpose, but it had also become a source of inspiration for countless others.

From that day forward, Benjamin continued to explore and add new pieces to his ever-evolving puzzle, for he knew that the journey of purpose was never truly complete. With each new addition, he discovered new depths within himself and unveiled new possibilities for making a positive impact on the world.

And so, the man who once felt adrift in the sea of possibilities became a guiding light, showing others the way to piece together their own puzzles of purpose. Benjamin's story reminds us that within the fragments of our passions, skills, and values lie the keys to creating a life that is deeply meaningful, fulfilling, and driven by a greater purpose.

2. Collaborative Visioning:

Enlist the help of a trusted friend or loved one for this exercise. Together, embark on a visioning journey where you each take turns sharing your passions, dreams, and aspirations. As you listen to your partner's aspirations, allow your imagination to soar and envision how your own passions can intertwine with theirs, creating a collaborative vision that transcends individual boundaries. Explore how your combined strengths and shared purpose can amplify impact and bring about profound positive change in the world.

In a world where dreams intertwine and possibilities abound, there lived a man named Daniel and a woman named Sophia. They were kindred spirits, united by a shared love for exploration, creativity, and a deep desire to make a meaningful impact on the world. Little did they know that their paths were about to converge in a powerful way, forever changing the course of their individual journeys.

Daniel and Sophia decided to embark on a collaborative visioning journey, drawing strength from their unwavering belief in the power of connection and the magic that emerges when two souls align their dreams. They gathered in a cosy café, their minds buzzing with anticipation and their hearts open to the infinite possibilities that lay before them.

They sat across from each other, their eyes sparkling with excitement, and began to take turns sharing their passions, dreams, and aspirations. As Sophia spoke of her desire to create sustainable art installations that would inspire environmental consciousness, Daniel's eyes widened in awe. His own vision of using technology to develop innovative solutions for clean energy aligned perfectly with Sophia's passion.

As they listened to each other's aspirations, a symphony of possibilities played in their minds. They allowed their imaginations to soar, envisioning how their unique passions and talents could intertwine, creating a collaborative vision that transcended their individual boundaries. Sophia's artistic skills combined with Daniel's technological expertise sparked a vision of captivating installations that not only showcased sustainable practices but also generated clean energy for the community.

With every exchange, their ideas became more vivid, more intertwined. They explored how their combined strengths could amplify their impact and bring about profound positive change in the world. They saw themselves collaborating with local artists, engineers, and environmentalists, forming a coalition of like-minded individuals who shared their vision for a more sustainable and harmonious future.

The energy in the café buzzed with excitement as Daniel and Sophia realised the tremendous potential of their collaborative vision. They knew they had found kindred spirits in each other, partners who would fuel their passion and push them to reach new heights. They pledged to embark on this journey together, bound by their shared purpose and their unwavering belief in the power of their collaborative vision.

Over time, Daniel and Sophia's collaborative vision blossomed into reality. They founded a creative collective that merged art, technology, and environmental consciousness, sparking a movement that captured the hearts and minds of people worldwide. Through their captivating installations and innovative solutions, they inspired communities to embrace sustainable practices and brought about tangible change in the world.

As their collaborative vision unfolded, Daniel and Sophia discovered that the true magic lay not only in the impact they made but also in the deep connection they forged with each other and with the world around them. They realised that when passion and purpose intertwine, and when souls come together in shared vision, remarkable things can happen.

Their story became an inspiration, a testament to the power of collaboration and the transformative potential that lies within us when we connect our dreams. Daniel and Sophia's journey reminded others that by seeking kindred spirits and engaging in collaborative visioning, we can amplify our impact, create profound positive change, and shape a future that reflects the beauty and harmony we envision.

And so, in the tapestry of their collaborative vision, Daniel and Sophia wove a story of inspiration, creativity, and environmental stewardship. Together, they proved that when two souls unite in a shared purpose, their dreams become unstoppable, and the world becomes a canvas for infinite possibility.

3. Soul's Map:

Take a quiet moment to sit in reflection and close your eyes. Allow your mind to wander as you imagine yourself as a courageous explorer, navigating the landscape of your soul. With each breath, envision a map unfolding before you—a map that holds the key to aligning your passions with your purpose. On this mystical map, mark the places that represent your passions, the crossroads that symbolise your core values, and the destinations that signify your desired impact. Let this soul's map guide you towards the intersections where passion and purpose converge.

In the mystical realm where wisdom and magic intertwined, there lived a humble seeker named Evangeline. Driven by an insatiable thirst for self-discovery, she yearned to navigate the depths of her soul and unlock the secrets that lay hidden within. Guided by the ancient alchemic texts, she embarked on a transformative journey that would forever alter the course of her life.

Evangeline followed the teachings of the alchemists, their words etched in her heart. She sought solace in a quiet room, closed her eyes, and allowed her mind to wander into the vast expanse of her own being. With each breath, she became a courageous explorer, venturing into uncharted territories within her soul.

As Evangeline delved deeper, she encountered a myriad of landscapes—each one a reflection of her experiences, emotions, and aspirations. She traversed the rolling hills of resilience, climbed the towering mountains of determination, and swam in the depths of self-compassion. The terrain shifted, sometimes treacherous and dark, other times bursting with vibrant hues of love and joy.

Amidst her soul's labyrinth, Evangeline discovered symbols and signs that spoke to her with profound wisdom. They appeared like ancient engravings on the walls of her subconscious, each carrying a message from the depths of her being. Guided by intuition, she deciphered the hidden meanings and crafted her soul's map—a testament to her inner landscape and a guide for her life's purpose.

Embracing the alchemic principles, Evangeline understood that within her soul's map lay the keys to transformation. She recognised the alchemical process as a metaphor for her own growth—a journey of refining and transmuting the raw materials of her being into something extraordinary.

In her quest for wisdom, Evangeline discovered that the true alchemy was not solely about personal transformation but also about the profound impact she could have on the world. She realised that her soul's map held the potential to inspire and guide others, igniting their own transformative journeys.

Filled with a newfound purpose, Evangeline shared her soul's map with those who sought guidance and solace. She unveiled its intricacies, weaving tales of resilience, determination, and self-compassion. Her wisdom resonated deeply with those who listened, lighting a spark within their own souls.

But, in an unexpected twist of fate, something extraordinary occurred. As Evangeline shared her soul's map, it began to change, adapting and expanding with each encounter. The engravings morphed and transformed, revealing new paths, hidden treasures, and unforeseen possibilities.

In this unanticipated outcome, Evangeline discovered the true nature of her soul's map. It was not meant to be static, but rather a living document, evolving and growing alongside her. As she embraced this revelation, her purpose expanded beyond her own journey—it became a vessel for collective transformation.

Evangeline's soul's map became a beacon of wisdom, guiding countless souls on their own quests for self-discovery. It inspired them to embark on their own courageous explorations, to seek the depths of their beings, and to transmute their own raw materials into something extraordinary.

And so, in the realm where wisdom and magic intertwined, Evangeline's journey merged with the collective, as her soul's map continued to evolve and illuminate the path for all who sought truth and transformation. Her story became a timeless testament to the power of self-reflection, wisdom, and the unexpected outcomes that can arise when we embark on the courageous journey of exploring the landscape of our souls.

Through these unconventional exercises, you will embark on a profound journey of self-discovery, visioning, and purpose alignment. The puzzle, collaborative visioning, and soul's map will be your compasses as you navigate the intricate tapestry that connects your passions to a greater purpose. Brace yourself for a voyage of self-realisation, where you will unlock the mysteries of your unique calling and unleash a life of meaning, fulfilment, and profound impact. Let us set forth on this extraordinary quest, where passion and purpose dance harmoniously in the symphony of your soul.

CHAPTER 5
OVERCOMING OBSTACLES

On the path to pursuing your passions, obstacles are bound to arise. In this chapter, we shine a light on the common challenges that may hinder the pursuit of your passions and provide practical strategies to overcome them. We'll explore ways to build resilience, cultivate a growth mindset, and develop effective problem-solving skills. With inspiring stories and insightful exercises, you'll gain the tools and mindset necessary to persist in the face of challenges and keep your passion aflame.

Greetings, resilient seeker, as you navigate the adventurous path towards your passions, it's inevitable that obstacles will emerge like riddles waiting to be solved. But fear not, for within these challenges lies an opportunity for growth and transformation. In this chapter, we illuminate the dimly lit corners where obstacles dwell, guiding you towards practical strategies and illuminating stories that will empower you to conquer any hurdle that comes your way. Get ready to build resilience, cultivate a growth mind-set, and embrace the art of problem-solving, as we equip you with the tools to keep your passion aflame, even amidst the fiercest storms.

Exercises:

1. The Power of Reframing:

Obstacles often appear daunting and insurmountable, but they are also catalysts for personal growth. In this exercise, choose one of your current obstacles and reframe it as an opportunity for learning and development. Ask yourself: What can I gain from this challenge? How can it help me become a stronger, wiser, and more resilient individual? Embrace a growth mindset and shift your perspective to see obstacles as steppingstones towards your ultimate success.

To put things in perspective: in the arid plains of a vast desert, a diligent dung beetle named Oliver rolled his dung ball with unwavering determination. It was his daily mission to gather food for himself and his community. One scorching day, as Oliver pushed his precious ball across the sandy dunes, an immense obstacle loomed before him—an enormous boulder blocking his path.

At first glance, the boulder appeared insurmountable. Oliver felt his determination waver as doubts crept into his mind. How could he, a tiny dung beetle, overcome such a colossal obstacle? But then, he remembered the wisdom of reframing, the power of seeing challenges as opportunities.

With a newfound perspective, Oliver paused and reflected. He asked himself, "What can I gain from this challenge? How can it help me become a stronger, wiser, and more resilient beetle?" As he pondered these questions, a spark of resilience ignited within him.

Oliver realised that the boulder was not merely an obstacle but an opportunity for growth. He saw it as a chance to develop his strength and determination, to expand his problem-solving skills, and to inspire his fellow dung beetles to persevere in the face of adversity.

Embracing a growth mindset, Oliver shifted his perspective. He saw the boulder not as an immovable blockade but as a steppingstone towards his ultimate success. With renewed determination, he devised a plan.

Oliver called upon his fellow dung beetles, sharing his newfound perspective, and enlisting their support. Together, they collaborated and brainstormed creative solutions. They harnessed their collective strength and wisdom, exploring different approaches to conquer the boulder.

With synchronised efforts and unwavering determination, the dung beetles united as a powerful force. They harnessed their strength and pushed against the boulder; their collective will be propelling them forward. Slowly but steadily, they inched the boulder, shifting its position and creating a pathway for Oliver's dung ball to pass through.

As they successfully manoeuvred the boulder, Oliver felt an overwhelming sense of triumph. The challenge that once appeared insurmountable had become a testament to their resilience, collaboration, and growth. Oliver realised that the obstacle had transformed him into a stronger, wiser, and more resilient dung beetle.

News of Oliver's triumph spread throughout the desert, inspiring other creatures to reframe their own obstacles. Oliver's story became a symbol of determination, reminding everyone that challenges, no matter how daunting, held within them the seeds of growth and personal development.

From that day forward, Oliver continued his journey with a renewed perspective. He embraced each obstacle as an opportunity for learning, development, and transformation. His unwavering spirit and the power of reframing became a beacon of inspiration for all who faced challenges along their own paths.

And so, in the vast desert, a tiny dung beetle named Oliver showed the world the transformative power of reframing. His story reminds us that within every obstacle lies the potential for growth, and that by embracing a growth mindset and shifting our perspective, we can turn even the most daunting challenges into steppingstones towards our ultimate success.

2. The Resilience Playlist:

Create a playlist of uplifting and empowering songs that inspire you to overcome challenges. These songs should ignite a fire within, reminding you of your strength, resilience, and unwavering determination. Whenever you face an obstacle, play your resilience playlist, and let the music infuse you with courage and motivation. Let the lyrics and melodies remind you that you are capable of surmounting any hurdle and that setbacks are merely temporary detours on your journey to success.

Once upon a time, in a land filled with laughter and music, there lived a quirky character named Harold. Harold was a peculiar fellow, known for his penchant for creating peculiar playlists. One day, as he stumbled upon the concept of a resilience playlist, an idea sparked in his mischievous mind.

With a mischievous grin, Harold set out to create the most unconventional resilience playlist the world had ever seen. He gathered his trusty kazoo, his grandmother's accordion, and an assortment of peculiar musical instruments. He was determined to compose a playlist that would uplift and empower not only himself but also anyone who dared to listen.

Harold's playlist was a chaotic symphony of unconventional sounds and unexpected lyrics. He began with a kazoo rendition of "Eye of the Tiger," followed by an accordion interpretation of "I Will Survive." He added in a quirky ukulele cover of "Don't Stop Believin'" and a cowbell-accompanied performance of "We Will Rock You."

With each song, Harold's enthusiasm grew. He channelled his unwavering determination into every note, filling the air with a cacophony of resilience. Passers-by couldn't help but stop and stare, their puzzled expressions slowly transforming into smiles and laughter. Harold's resilience playlist had an unexpected effect—it ignited joy and laughter in the hearts of all who listened.

As Harold continued his impromptu concert, an old man named Arthur, known for his grumpy demeanour, wandered by. Arthur was known as the town's resident grouch, his frown etched permanently on his face. But as the sounds of Harold's unconventional resilience playlist reached his ears, Arthur's expression shifted. A faint smile tugged at the corners of his mouth, and his foot tapped in rhythm to the lively tunes.

In a moment of spontaneity, Arthur joined Harold in his musical escapade. He grabbed a pair of wooden spoons and began drumming along with the beat. The sight of the grumpy old man grooving to the peculiar melodies brought laughter and cheer to everyone around.

From that day forward, Harold's resilience playlist became a symbol of laughter, resilience, and the unexpected power of music. People from all walks of life embraced the joyous melodies, creating their own peculiar interpretations of the songs. Laughter filled the streets, and the town's spirit soared to new heights.

And so, the peculiar playlist, composed of unconventional sounds and unexpected lyrics, not only ignited a fire of resilience within Harold but also spread laughter and joy far and wide. It reminded everyone that in the face of challenges, embracing humour and finding joy in the unexpected can be the key to overcoming obstacles and rediscovering the strength within.

And as the peculiar playlist continued to echo through the town, Harold's music inspired a movement of resilience, laughter, and a newfound appreciation for the power of the unexpected. For in the world of peculiar playlists, where laughter and resilience converge, anything is possible— even finding the strength to conquer life's challenges with a smile on your face and a song in your heart.

I just want to point out it is always worth having a couple of kazoos. Try making someone laugh when they have a kazoo in their mouth… It is ridiculous! Anyway, I wanted to bring in a kazoo to this writing... Thought you might like to know that!

3. Collaborative Problem-Solving:

Engage in collaborative problem-solving by seeking support from a trusted friend or mentor. Share one of your current obstacles with them and invite their insights and perspectives. Together, brainstorm creative solutions and approaches that you may not have considered on your own. Embrace the power of collective wisdom and let their input inspire new ideas and possibilities. By leveraging the strength of collaboration, you will discover innovative pathways to overcome obstacles and keep your passion alive.

Here's a story that embodies the spirit of collaborative problem-solving and showcases how a mentor or trusted friend can have a revelation that leads to a positive outcome:

In a small village nestled among rolling hills, there lived a wise old woman named Elisa. With her years of experience and a heart full of compassion, she had become a trusted mentor to the villagers. One day, as the village faced a perplexing problem, Elisa was called upon to guide them through a collaborative problem-solving session.

The issue at hand was a stubborn drought that had plagued the village, leaving crops withered and spirits low. The villagers, seeking a resolution, gathered in the town square, hoping that their collective efforts would lead to a breakthrough. Elisa stood before them, her eyes filled with wisdom and her voice resonating with calm assurance.

The collaborative problem-solving session began as villagers shared their concerns, ideas, and observations. As the discussions unfolded, Elisa listened intently, offering gentle guidance, and encouraging open dialogue. The atmosphere buzzed with the energy of collective brainstorming, as the villagers explored various avenues and potential solutions.

As the day progressed, Elisa's trusted friend, a farmer named Samuel, quietly observed the discussions. Samuel had spent his life tending the land, intimately familiar with the rhythms of nature. Despite his initial reluctance to speak up, a spark of realisation ignited within him.

With a newfound sense of urgency, Samuel approached Elisa, sharing his revelation. He had noticed an ancient well, long forgotten, nestled deep in the heart of the village. Through years of drought, it had remained untapped and hidden. Samuel believed that this well could hold the key to solving the village's water scarcity.

Elisa's eyes widened with surprise and gratitude. She had missed this crucial piece of information. The collaborative problem-solving session took a sudden turn as Samuel's revelation brought renewed hope to the villagers.

With Samuel's guidance, the villagers gathered around the forgotten well. Together, they worked tirelessly to restore it, clearing debris, and digging channels to bring the water to the thirsty fields. As they laboured, their shared purpose and determination fuelled their efforts, creating a sense of unity that transcended individual boundaries.

Soon, water once again flowed from the ancient well, nourishing the parched land. The fields began to flourish, bringing relief and abundance to the village. The collaborative problem-solving session had not only resolved the drought but also strengthened the bond between the villagers and rejuvenated their spirits.

Elisa marvelled at the power of collaborative problem-solving and the wisdom that could emerge from unexpected sources. Samuel's revelation had been a turning point, highlighting the importance of actively listening to all voices and embracing the collective wisdom of the community.

The village rejoiced, not only for the restored water supply but also for the reminder that solutions can arise when people come together, pooling their knowledge and experiences. The mentor and trusted friend, Elisa, learned an invaluable lesson from Samuel. She recognised that wisdom could manifest in unexpected places, and that a mentor's role often extended beyond guiding to also learning and being open to revelations.

As the village thrived and the bonds between the villagers grew stronger, Elisa and Samuel became a symbol of collaborative problem-solving and the transformative power of mentorship. Their story echoed through generations, inspiring others to seek guidance, embrace collective wisdom, and remain open to unexpected revelations that could lead to positive outcomes.

And so, in the small village, the spirit of collaboration and mentorship shone brightly, reminding all who listened that when minds come together in pursuit of a shared goal, remarkable solutions can emerge, and the power of revelation can bring about positive change that reverberates through the hearts of a community.

Through these transformative exercises, you will develop the resilience, growth mindset, and problem-solving skills necessary to conquer any obstacle that comes your way. Embrace the power of reframing, let the melodies of your resilience playlist fuel your determination, and tap into the collective wisdom of collaborative problem-solving. With these tools in hand, you'll navigate the twists and turns of your journey with confidence and grace, emerging stronger and more determined to keep your passion aflame.

So, intrepid seeker, prepare yourself for the exhilarating adventure that lies ahead. Embrace the challenges as opportunities, let the music of resilience carry you through, and open your heart to the collective wisdom that surrounds you. Together, we will conquer the obstacles and illuminate the path towards a life of unwavering passion and purpose.

PART 2
WEALTH AS WONDER

Step into the realm of abundance and wonder as we embark on Part 2 of our journey—Wealth as Wonder. In this chapter, we invite you to challenge conventional notions of wealth and delve into a broader understanding of what it truly means to live a rich and fulfilling life.

We begin by rethinking wealth, inviting you to shift your mindset and expand your definition beyond material possessions. True wealth encompasses the treasures of experience, connection, and personal growth. It is the richness found in moments of joy, love, and purpose that transcend the confines of mere possessions.

As we navigate this transformative path, we embrace gratitude as a guiding light. Cultivating a practice of gratitude opens the floodgates of abundance, shifting our focus from scarcity to the bountiful blessings that surround us. By acknowledging and appreciating the present moment, we unlock the limitless potential that awaits us.

Embracing an abundance mentality is our next endeavour. We liberate ourselves from the constraints of scarcity thinking, recognising that there is enough for everyone. Abundance is not a finite resource; it is an expansive mindset that opens doors to greater opportunities, collaboration, and the co-creation of a thriving world.

Through thought-provoking insights and practical exercises, we embark on a journey of discovery, challenging old paradigms and opening ourselves to the wonders of true wealth. So, let us embrace the magic that unfolds when we redefine wealth, cultivate gratitude, and adopt an abundance mentality. Get ready to embark on a path where wealth becomes an enchanting tapestry of experiences, connections, and limitless possibilities.

With open hearts and minds, we step into the realm of wealth as wonder, ready to explore the depths of abundance that await us. Let the journey begin!

CHAPTER 6
RETHINKING WEALTH

Shifting your mind-set and expanding your definition of wealth to encompass more than just material possessions.

Welcome to the extraordinary realm of rethinking wealth—a journey that takes us beyond the confines of material possessions and into the vast expanse of abundance that awaits us. In this chapter, we embark on a transformative exploration, challenging traditional notions and expanding our definition of wealth to encompass the intangible treasures that shape our lives.

In a world often fixated on accumulating material riches, we dare to ask a different question: What if true wealth extends far beyond the boundaries of possessions? What if it resides in the moments that touch our hearts, the connections that nourish our souls, and the experiences that ignite our spirits?

As we venture into this uncharted territory, we set forth on a path of empowerment and liberation. We release the grip of consumerism and embrace a mindset that allows us to appreciate the richness that lies within and around us. It is a paradigm shift that propels us towards a life of abundance and fulfilment.

Rethinking wealth begins with the realisation that our worth and well-being are not defined solely by material acquisitions. It requires us to delve deeper, to explore the intricacies of our human experience, and to discover the boundless treasures that go beyond what can be measured or owned.

Within the tapestry of wealth, we find the vibrant threads of love, compassion, purpose, and joy. We discover the wealth of cherished relationships, the richness of shared experiences, and the abundance of personal growth and self-discovery. We uncover the profound value of giving back and making a positive impact on the world around us.

As we embark on this transformative journey, we open our hearts and minds to the vast possibilities that lie before us. We embrace the wealth that resides in the beauty of nature, the wisdom of mentors, the simple pleasures of life, and the moments of awe that take our breath away.

Let us expand our horizons, challenge the status quo, and reimagine what it means to be truly wealthy. By shifting our mindset and broadening our definition of wealth, we invite a newfound sense of abundance into our lives—a wealth that transcends material possessions and permeates every aspect of our being.

So, dear traveller, as we embark on this extraordinary quest, let us walk hand in hand, ready to uncover the immeasurable wealth that awaits us. Together, we shall redefine the meaning of abundance and embrace the intangible treasures that enrich our souls. Let us embark on this journey of rethinking wealth, and may our hearts be forever open to the wonders that lie ahead.

Here are three fun and unconventional exercises to help you rethink wealth and expand your definition beyond material possessions:

1. The Gratitude Treasure Hunt:

Embark on a gratitude treasure hunt to discover the hidden gems of wealth in your life. Create a list of non-material things you are grateful for, such as experiences, relationships, personal qualities, or moments of joy. Then, go on a playful adventure to find tangible representations or symbols of these intangible treasures. For example, if you're grateful for the joy of laughter, find a small item that reminds you of laughter and keep it as a physical reminder of this precious wealth. As you gather these symbolic treasures, reflect on the abundance that exists beyond material possessions and how these treasures enrich your life.

Once upon a time, in a whimsical town known as Joyville, the townsfolk were buzzing with excitement over a remarkable event—the Gratitude Treasure Hunt. It was a playful adventure that celebrated the magic of gratitude and the hidden treasures of abundance.

On a bright sunny morning, the townspeople gathered at the town square, donning colourful hats, and carrying treasure maps filled with gratitude prompts. The air was charged with anticipation as the adventure was about to begin.

Leading the expedition was an enthusiastic and lively guide named Oliver. With a twinkle in his eye, he addressed the crowd, "Welcome, dear adventurers, to the Gratitude Treasure Hunt! Today, we embark on a quest to discover the treasures of abundance that surround us. Are you ready?"

The crowd erupted in cheers and nods, ready to unlock the secrets of gratitude. Oliver handed out magnifying glasses and tiny treasure chests to each participant, explaining that these would be their tools to collect the intangible treasures they would encounter.

The first clue led them to a serene garden, where they were instructed to find the "Whispering Petals of Appreciation." As the adventurers wandered through the fragrant blooms, they listened intently. Suddenly, a gentle breeze swept through the garden, carrying whispers of gratitude from the flowers themselves. The treasure chests were filled with invisible petals, representing the gratitude that bloomed within their hearts.

The next clue guided them to a bustling café, where they were tasked with finding the "Melodies of Kindness." The adventurers sat at tables, sipping warm drinks and engaging in heart-warming conversations. Suddenly, the café's talented musicians began playing uplifting tunes, filling the air with melodies that touched the souls of all present. The adventurers used their magnifying glasses to capture invisible musical notes, depositing them into their treasure chests.

The final clue led them to a picturesque lakeside, where they were challenged to find the "Sparkling Ripples of Joy." Excitement filled the air as the adventurers gathered by the water's edge. They skipped stones, shared laughter, and embraced the beauty of the moment. Suddenly, the lake shimmered with vibrant colours, reflecting the collective joy that emanated from their hearts. The adventurers captured these invisible ripples in their treasure chests, their chests now brimming with gratitude and joy.

Returning to the town square, the adventurers opened their treasure chests, revealing the invisible treasures they had collected. A wave of awe and gratitude washed over the crowd as they witnessed the magic of intangible wealth. The invisible petals, musical notes, and sparkling ripples had transformed into vibrant, tangible representations of abundance.

Oliver beamed with pride, his eyes glistening. "Congratulations, dear adventurers! You have discovered the true treasures of gratitude. May these reminders of abundance inspire you to see the richness that lies within and around you."

The townspeople rejoiced, carrying their newfound treasures of gratitude with them as they ventured forth in life. From that day forward, the Gratitude Treasure Hunt became an annual tradition in Joyville, a joyful reminder that the greatest treasures are often unseen but deeply felt.

And so, in the magical town of Joyville, the adventure of the Gratitude Treasure Hunt continued to weave its enchanting spell, reminding all who embarked on the quest that gratitude unlocks the hidden treasures of abundance and fills life with immeasurable joy.

2. Story Swap:

Gather a group of friends or loved ones and engage in a lively story swap. Each person takes turns sharing a personal story that highlights a moment of wealth and abundance in their life that has nothing to do with material possessions. It could be a tale of love, a moment of profound connection, a personal achievement, or an act of kindness. As each story unfolds, pay close attention to the emotions and experiences shared, and let it inspire you to broaden your perspective on what true wealth means. This exercise encourages you to recognise and celebrate the richness of life's non-material treasures.

Once upon a time, in a cosy cottage nestled amidst a vibrant meadow, a group of friends gathered for an enchanting evening of storytelling. They had decided to embark on a delightful adventure known as a Story Swap, where each person would share a tale close to their heart.

The room was adorned with flickering candles, casting a warm glow upon the eager faces that awaited their turn to captivate and inspire. Emily, the host of the evening, sat in a circle with her friends, eager to embark on this magical storytelling journey.

The fire crackled in the hearth as Emily began the evening, setting the tone with a whimsical tale of an adventurous bunny who dared to explore a mystical forest. Her story was filled with laughter, suspense, and valuable life lessons. The room came alive with vivid imaginations and eager anticipation for the stories yet to come.

Next in line was Thomas, a wise old soul with a twinkle in his eye. He shared a heartfelt story of a young musician who discovered the power of his melodies to heal and unite people from all walks of life. The room fell silent, deeply moved by the transformative power of music portrayed in Thomas's tale.

As the evening progressed, stories of courage, love, and resilience filled the air. Sarah, a spirited traveller, enchanted the group with her account of a daring journey through exotic lands, where she encountered magical creatures and learned the true meaning of bravery. Each story revealed a unique perspective, weaving together a tapestry of emotions and insights.

Amidst the laughter and heartfelt applause, it was Lily's turn. Lily was known for her boundless imagination and love for fairy tales. With a mischievous smile, she transported the group into a whimsical realm, where talking animals and enchanted forests were the norm. Her story unfolded with wonder and joy, leaving everyone enchanted and eager for more.

The evening continued with each member of the group sharing their cherished stories. From tales of personal triumph to stories passed down through generations, the room resonated with a sense of connection and shared wisdom.

As the night drew to a close, Emily thanked her friends for their beautiful contributions, acknowledging the power of storytelling to unite hearts and ignite the imagination. The Story Swap had not only entertained and enlightened but had also deepened the bonds between these friends.

In the days that followed, the magic of the Story Swap lingered within their hearts. Inspired by the tales they had heard, the friends embarked on new adventures, chased their dreams with renewed vigour, and embraced the beauty of storytelling in their everyday lives.

And so, in that cosy cottage surrounded by nature's embrace, the tradition of the Story Swap continued. It became a cherished gathering where tales were spun, memories were forged, and the power of storytelling continued to illuminate the path of friendship and self-discovery.

For in the art of storytelling, the threads of imagination, empathy, and connection intertwine, creating a tapestry of shared experiences. The Story Swap had reminded these friends of the magic that lies within each narrative, waiting to be shared and celebrated.

And so, dear reader, may you too gather your loved ones, ignite the spark of imagination, and embark on your own Story Swap. Let the tales enchant, inspire, and illuminate the path of your own unique journey. For in the power of storytelling, we discover the extraordinary within the ordinary and the extraordinary within ourselves.

3. Abundance Vision Board:

Create an abundance vision board that focuses on non-material aspects of wealth. Collect images, words, and symbols that represent the different facets of wealth beyond possessions—experiences, personal growth, relationships, and contribution. Assemble these elements on a vision board, arranging them in a way that resonates with you. Display it prominently in your living space as a daily reminder to shift your mind-set and expand your definition of wealth. Let your abundance vision board serve as a visual affirmation of the multifaceted riches that exist beyond material possessions and inspire you to seek and appreciate them.

Once upon a time, in a quaint village nestled among rolling hills, there lived a wise old woman named Amelia. She possessed a unique ability to see beyond the surface of things and guide others towards a deeper understanding of life's mysteries. One day, Amelia invited a group of curious villagers to join her in an exploration of abundance through the creation of an Abundance Vision Board.

Gathered in Amelia's cosy cottage, the villagers eagerly embraced the opportunity to expand their notion of wealth beyond material possessions. With scissors, glue, and a collection of magazines, they embarked on a journey of self-reflection and creative expression.

As the villagers leafed through the magazines, they sought out images and words that represented the non-material aspects of wealth—love, fulfilment, inner peace, connection, and personal growth. They crafted their vision boards with care, arranging the chosen elements in a way that resonated deeply within their souls.

Amelia, observing the villagers' process, shared her wisdom. "Dear friends, as you create your Abundance Vision Boards, remember that true wealth lies not in what we possess, but in the experiences, relationships, and inner qualities that bring joy and fulfilment. Let your vision boards reflect the essence of abundance that resides within you."

As the villagers immersed themselves in the creative process, an unexpected twist occurred. As they arranged the images and words on their boards, they noticed that their visions seemed to intermingle and merge, forming a vibrant mosaic of shared aspirations. It was as if their individual visions were intricately connected, creating a collective vision of abundance that transcended their individual boundaries.

Amelia, with a knowing smile, whispered, "Deep insights often arise from the interplay of our unique journeys. Your Abundance Vision Boards have become a reflection not only of your individual desires but also of your shared aspirations. This is a reminder that we are all connected, and together we can create a tapestry of abundance that enriches us all."

In that moment, the villagers felt a profound shift within their hearts. They realised that their visions were not separate, but threads woven together to form a collective dream of a harmonious and abundant community.

As the years passed, the villagers continued to gaze upon their Abundance Vision Boards, drawing inspiration from their shared vision. They collaborated, supporting one another's aspirations and endeavours, and the village blossomed into a vibrant hub of creativity, love, and connection. The abundance they sought was not solely individual; it was a tapestry that encompassed the entire community.

And so, the Abundance Vision Boards became more than just creative collages. They became powerful reminders of the interconnectedness of dreams and the transformative power of shared vision. The villagers discovered that true abundance lay not only in personal fulfilment but in the joy of collective growth and the ripple effect of their positive contributions.

Amelia, their wise guide, watched with a sense of fulfilment. She had witnessed the villagers embrace the deeper meaning of abundance, transcending the confines of material possessions. Through their Abundance Vision Boards, they had tapped into the wellspring of wisdom within, recognising the interconnected nature of their dreams and the boundless possibilities that arise when individuals unite with a shared vision.

And so, dear reader, may you too be inspired to create your own Abundance Vision Board, reflecting the non-material aspects of wealth that resonate with your soul. May you discover the unexpected insights and interconnectedness that emerge when individual dreams unite in a collective vision. Embrace the transformative power of shared aspirations and let the tapestry of abundance unfold in your life and the lives of those around you.

These exercises encourage you to step beyond the conventional boundaries of material wealth and explore the vast array of riches that exist in the intangible aspects of life. Through gratitude, storytelling, and visual representation, you can expand your perspective, celebrating the non-material treasures that contribute to a truly fulfilling and abundant existence.

CHAPTER 7
CULTIVATING GRATITUDE
EMBRACING GRATITUDE AS A TRANSFORMATIVE PRACTICE

Welcome to a chapter filled with the radiant power of gratitude, where we explore the transformative practice that has the ability to shape our lives in remarkable ways. Cultivating gratitude is not merely an act of appreciation; it is a profound and sacred journey that opens the doors to abundance and invites greater opportunities into our existence.

In a world that often rushes by in a whirlwind of busyness and demands, it is easy to overlook the blessings that surround us. Yet, by embracing gratitude as a daily practice, we awaken to the infinite gifts that grace our lives—the gifts of love, connection, and the simple joys that weave the tapestry of our existence.

As we embark on this transformative path, we are reminded that gratitude is not limited to grand gestures or extravagant events. It is in the moments of quiet reflection, in the whispers of gratitude for the ordinary miracles that grace our days. It is the acknowledgment of the sunlight streaming through a window, the embrace of a loved one, or the taste of a warm meal that nourishes both body and soul.

When we cultivate gratitude, we shift our perspective from scarcity to abundance. We free ourselves from the grip of longing and dissatisfaction, and instead, embrace the richness of what already resides within us and surrounds us. Gratitude becomes a beacon of light, illuminating the path to contentment and attracting greater blessings into our lives.

Moreover, the transformative power of gratitude extends beyond our personal sphere. It radiates outward, touching the lives of those around us. As we express gratitude, we inspire a ripple effect of positivity, opening hearts and fostering deeper connections. Gratitude becomes a bridge that unites souls, creating a shared experience of abundance and joy.

In the pages that follow, we will delve into the profound practices of cultivating gratitude. We will explore rituals, exercises, and reflections that will awaken your awareness and deepen your gratitude practice. Prepare to be amazed by the countless blessings that unfold as you open your heart to the transformative power of gratitude.

So, dear seeker of abundance and joy, let us embark on this sacred journey of cultivating gratitude. May it infuse your life with a profound sense of appreciation, illuminate the blessings that lie within and around you, and pave the way for a future filled with endless possibilities. Together, let us embrace the transformative practice of gratitude and unlock the doors to a life of abundance.

Here are three fun exercises for cultivating gratitude that offer a unique twist:

1. Gratitude Dot-to-Dot:

Engage in a playful exercise of connecting the dots to reveal a gratitude-inspired image. Instead of a traditional dot-to-dot with numbers, use gratitude-themed words or phrases as the connection points. Each time you connect two dots, take a moment to reflect on something you are grateful for that aligns with the word or phrase. As the image slowly emerges, let it serve as a visual representation of the many blessings in your life, reminding you of the abundance that surrounds you.

Once upon a time, in the colourful village of Gratiaville, the residents were buzzing with excitement over a special event—the Gratitude Dot-to-Dot Extravaganza. It was a playful celebration of gratitude where the villagers came together to connect the dots and reveal a heart-warming image that embodied their collective appreciation.

The village square was adorned with vibrant decorations, and a large canvas was spread out on a wooden easel. Villagers of all ages eagerly gathered around, clutching their dot-to-dot sheets filled with gratitude-themed words. The anticipation was palpable as they prepared to embark on this unique journey of thankfulness.

As the event began, the village mayor, Mr. Grateful, took to the stage with a cheerful smile. "Welcome, dear friends, to the Gratitude Dot-to-Dot Extravaganza! Today, we come together to celebrate the power of gratitude and unveil a beautiful image that represents our collective appreciation."

The villagers huddled around the dot-to-dot canvas, ready to connect the dots. Instead of the usual numbered dots, however, they discovered something unexpected. Each dot on the canvas was intricately shaped like a miniature door.

Perplexed yet intrigued, the villagers exchanged curious glances but embraced the challenge with open hearts. They started connecting the dots, each door leading to a different gratitude-themed surprise.

The first door-dotted line led to a small note that read, "Grateful for Unexpected Kindness." The villagers smiled, recounting moments when strangers had shown them kindness, like someone helping carry groceries or offering a warm smile on a gloomy day.

As they continued connecting the dots, they encountered more surprises. One dot led to a tiny envelope that held a handwritten message: "Grateful for Serendipitous Encounters." The villagers reminisced about chance meetings that had brought joy and inspiration into their lives, such as striking up a conversation with a like-minded soul or discovering a hidden gem in the village.

With every connection, the villagers uncovered gratitude-themed surprises they had never expected. They discovered gratitude for simple pleasures, like the aroma of freshly baked bread, the laughter of children, and the soothing sound of raindrops on leaves. Each dot-to-dot connection revealed a precious moment of gratitude that touched their hearts.

As the final dot was connected, the image on the canvas slowly emerged—an intricate mosaic of intertwined hearts. The villagers gasped in awe, realising that the unexpected dots had created a masterpiece of interconnectedness and shared gratitude.

The village square echoed with applause and joyful laughter as the villagers celebrated their collective expression of appreciation. They realised that gratitude wasn't just about big gestures or grand experiences; it was about finding beauty in the unexpected, connecting the dots of gratitude that lay scattered throughout their lives.

From that day forward, the Gratitude Dot-to-Dot Extravaganza became an annual tradition in Gratiaville. The villagers continued to celebrate the unexpected dots of gratitude that adorned their canvas, cherishing the moments and connections that enriched their lives.

And so, in the village of Gratiaville, the spirit of gratitude lived on. The unexpected dots of gratitude served as a reminder to seek and appreciate the little surprises that brightened their days. Through the Gratitude Dot-to-Dot Extravaganza, the villagers discovered that gratitude was a mosaic of interconnected moments, filling their lives with joy, unity, and a deep appreciation for the wonders that lie within and around them.

2. Gratitude Jar of Moments:

Create a special gratitude jar that will serve as a repository for memorable moments of gratitude. Find a beautiful jar and decorate it in a way that resonates with you. Throughout each day, write down on colourful slips of paper the moments, experiences, or interactions that fill you with gratitude. It can be as simple as a kind gesture from a stranger, a moment of connection with a loved one, or an accomplishment you're proud of. Fill the jar with these slips of gratitude, and revisit them whenever you need a reminder of the abundant blessings in your life.

A little story…

In the small town of Evergreen, nestled amidst towering trees and picturesque landscapes, there lived a curious and adventurous soul named Alex. One sunny afternoon, while exploring the attic of an old Victorian house that had long been abandoned, Alex stumbled upon a dusty box tucked away in a forgotten corner.

With eyes full of curiosity, Alex opened the box and discovered a collection of colourful slips of paper neatly folded inside. On closer inspection, Alex realised that these were messages of gratitude, meticulously preserved over the years in what appeared to be a gratitude jar.

Intrigued by this unexpected find, Alex carefully unfolded the first slip of paper. It read, "Grateful for the laughter shared with loved ones on a rainy Sunday afternoon." Alex couldn't help but smile at the heartfelt sentiment captured in those few words. It was as if the writer's joy had been imprinted on the paper, waiting to be discovered and embraced once again.

Curiosity piqued, Alex continued unravelling the collection of gratitude notes, each containing a precious moment frozen in time. The gratitude jar had become a time capsule, preserving the profound insights and heartfelt expressions of gratitude from the past.

One slip of paper revealed gratitude for a simple act of kindness from a stranger, another for the beauty of a breath-taking sunset that painted the sky in hues of gold and pink. There were expressions of appreciation for moments of personal growth, for the embrace of a loved one during times of hardship, and for the unwavering support of friends who had become family.

As Alex delved deeper into the gratitude jar, a realisation dawned—the profound insights contained within these notes were not only a reflection of individual experiences but also a testament to the interconnectedness of human emotions and experiences. They were reminders that gratitude transcended time, age, and circumstance, bridging the gaps between generations and affirming the universality of gratitude as a transformative force.

With each gratitude note read, Alex felt a surge of inspiration and a renewed appreciation for the beauty and significance of gratitude in everyday life. The gratitude jar had become a treasure trove of wisdom, inviting Alex to reflect on the importance of embracing gratitude as a guiding principle for a fulfilling and purposeful existence.

With a sense of reverence, Alex carefully returned the slips of gratitude to the jar, preserving this treasure of insights for future explorers to discover. The gratitude jar had found a new custodian, one who understood the profound impact of gratitude and was eager to carry its transformative power forward.

From that day on, Alex embarked on a personal journey, incorporating the practice of gratitude into daily life. Inspired by the messages found in the gratitude jar, Alex began to notice and cherish the small moments of beauty, kindness, and growth that had often gone unnoticed before.

The profound insights contained within the gratitude jar became a guiding light, reminding Alex to pause, reflect, and express gratitude for the blessings woven throughout the tapestry of life. Through the gratitude jar's timeless wisdom, Alex discovered that even the simplest expressions of gratitude could spark joy, deepen connections, and transform the ordinary into the extraordinary.

And so, dear reader, may the story of the gratitude jar inspire you to cultivate a practice of gratitude in your own life. Embrace the profound insights and the transformative power of gratitude, for within the folds of appreciation lie the keys to unlocking a life rich with meaning, connection, and unending abundance.

3. Gratitude Walk:

Take a mindful walk-in nature, immersing yourself in the beauty and serenity of your surroundings. As you stroll, intentionally focus on gratitude. With each step, express gratitude for something you observe—a blooming flower, a gentle breeze, or the soothing sounds of birdsong. Let your gratitude expand beyond nature and extend to various aspects of your life, acknowledging the blessings that come to mind. This exercise allows you to combine the practice of mindfulness with gratitude, fostering a deeper appreciation for the present moment and the wonders that surround you.

In the tranquil town of Serenity Springs, nestled amidst lush greenery and winding trails, lived a woman named Maya. Despite the serene surroundings, Maya often found herself caught in the whirlwind of daily responsibilities, feeling disconnected from the beauty and abundance that surrounded her.

One day, feeling overwhelmed and yearning for a shift in perspective, Maya decided to embark on a Gratitude Walk—an intentional journey of mindfulness and appreciation. With each step, she aimed to cultivate a deeper sense of gratitude for the present moment and the wonders that awaited her.

As Maya set foot on the winding path that led into the heart of nature, a gentle breeze brushed against her cheeks, as if whispering words of encouragement. The rustling leaves and melodic chirping of birds created a harmonious symphony that resonated within her soul.

With every mindful step, Maya began to notice the intricacies of her surroundings—the vibrant hues of wildflowers, the gentle babbling of a nearby brook, and the dance of sunlight filtering through the swaying trees. Her senses awakened to the rich tapestry of nature's offerings, and a newfound appreciation for the world around her emerged.

As Maya continued her Gratitude Walk, she shifted her focus to her own experiences and blessings. With each breath, she expressed gratitude for her health, her loved ones, and the opportunities that had shaped her journey. She acknowledged the challenges she had overcome, recognising the strength and resilience that had carried her through.

In the depths of her gratitude, Maya felt a profound shift within. She realised that gratitude was not just an expression of appreciation; it was a state of being—a lens through which she could perceive the world. With gratitude as her guide, she saw beauty where she once saw mundanity, abundance where she once saw scarcity, and opportunity where she once saw obstacles.

As Maya reached the end of her Gratitude Walk, she paused, a serene smile gracing her lips. She felt a profound connection to the world around her, as if nature had embraced her with open arms. Gratitude had opened her heart to the extraordinary in the ordinary, and she knew that this newfound perspective would permeate every aspect of her life.

From that day forward, Maya incorporated Gratitude Walks into her routine, finding solace and inspiration in the sanctuary of nature. With each walk, she continued to cultivate a deep sense of appreciation, allowing gratitude to infuse her days with joy, wonder, and an unwavering appreciation for the blessings that flowed through her life.

Maya's experience with the Gratitude Walk had a profound impact on her overall well-being. It taught her the power of mindfulness and the transformative potential of gratitude. Through this simple practice, she had discovered a gateway to inner peace, contentment, and an unwavering sense of abundance.

And so, dear reader, may Maya's story inspire you to embark on your own Gratitude Walk. As you wander amidst the beauty of nature, let each step be an opportunity to immerse yourself in the present moment, expressing heartfelt gratitude for the wonders that surround you. Allow gratitude to awaken your senses, shift your perspective, and transform your life, one grateful step at a time.

These unique exercises offer fresh approaches to cultivating gratitude, helping you deepen your practice and discover new perspectives. They encourage you to engage your senses, ignite your creativity, and infuse gratitude into your daily life in unexpected ways. Embrace these exercises as invitations to explore the transformative power of gratitude and unlock the doors to greater opportunities and abundance.

CHAPTER 8
EMBRACING ABUNDANCE MENTALITY: CULTIVATING A MIND-SET OF ABUNDANCE

Welcome to a transformative section that invites you to embrace the abundant nature of life and cultivate a mind-set that transcends scarcity. In this exploration of embracing abundance mentality, we delve into the profound understanding that there is enough for everyone—a boundless wellspring of opportunities, love, and resources that is not confined by limitations.

In a world often consumed by scarcity thinking, where fear and competition can overshadow our innate sense of abundance, it is vital to embark on a journey of reimagining our relationship with the abundance that surrounds us. By shifting our mind-set and embracing the belief that abundance is our birthright, we open ourselves to a vast realm of possibilities and create a ripple effect of prosperity in our lives and the lives of those around us.

Throughout this section, we will unravel the layers of scarcity thinking, challenge limiting beliefs, and offer transformative insights to nurture the seeds of abundance within. It is a call to reframe our perception of lack, replacing it with the recognition of the abundance that permeates every aspect of our existence.

As we dive deeper into the exploration of embracing abundance mentality, we discover that abundance is not solely measured by material possessions. It is a state of being—an expansive way of perceiving and experiencing life that extends beyond tangible resources. It is a mindset that allows us to recognise the abundance of love, creativity, joy, and connection that flows through our lives, fostering a deep sense of gratitude and fulfilment.

By embracing abundance mentality, we become conscious creators, recognising that our thoughts, intentions, and actions have the power to shape our reality. As we release the grip of scarcity thinking, we tap into the infinite well of abundance within, accessing the reservoir of potential that exists within each and every one of us.

Throughout the pages that follow, we will explore practical tools, insightful reflections, and empowering practices that will guide you on your journey toward embracing abundance mentality. Prepare to challenge your beliefs, expand your perception, and tap into the wellspring of abundance that is your birthright.

So, dear seeker of abundance and possibility, let us embark on this transformative exploration of embracing abundance mentality. Together, let us dispel the illusion of scarcity and open our hearts and minds to the ever-flowing current of abundance that flows through the tapestry of existence. By embracing abundance, we step into our power as co-creators of a world where there is enough for everyone, and where prosperity becomes a shared experience.

Here are three practical tools to help you embrace abundance mentality and cultivate a mindset of abundance:

1. Abundance Affirmations:

Create a list of empowering affirmations that reinforce the belief in abundance and dispel scarcity thinking. Write down statements that resonate with you, such as "I am a magnet for abundance," "The universe is abundant, and I am deserving of its blessings," or "There is always enough to go around." Repeat these affirmations daily, preferably in the morning or before bedtime, allowing them to permeate your subconscious mind and reinforce your belief in abundance. Over time, these affirmations will help rewire your thought patterns, replacing scarcity with abundance.

2. Gratitude Journal:

Dedicate a gratitude journal specifically to document the abundance in your life. Each day, write down at least three things you are grateful for, focusing on the non-material aspects of abundance, such as love, relationships, personal growth, or moments of joy. As you consistently practice gratitude, you will become more attuned to the abundant blessings that surround you, cultivating a sense of appreciation and expanding your perception of abundance. Reflecting on your gratitude journal during challenging times can serve as a powerful reminder of the abundance that has already manifested in your life.

3. Act of Generosity:

Engage in an act of generosity that aligns with your resources and abilities. It could be as simple as offering a kind word or gesture to someone in need, volunteering your time and skills for a cause you believe in, or sharing your knowledge and expertise to uplift others. By consciously engaging in acts of generosity, you shift your focus from scarcity to abundance, recognising that you have something valuable to offer to the world. This practice not only cultivates a mindset of abundance but also creates a ripple effect of positivity, opening doors for greater opportunities and connections.

These practical tools serve as steppingstones on your journey toward embracing abundance mentality. By consistently affirming abundance, practicing gratitude, and engaging in acts of generosity, you reframe your perception of scarcity and consciously align with the abundance that permeates every aspect of life. Embrace these tools with intention and an open heart, allowing them to support your transformative journey toward embracing abundance and recognising that there is enough for everyone.

Once upon a time, in the bustling city of Prosperia, there lived a man named Ethan and a woman named Lily. Both had been grappling with scarcity thinking, feeling trapped in a cycle of limited beliefs that hindered their ability to embrace abundance. Little did they know that their paths were about to intersect, setting in motion a transformative journey of embracing abundance mentality.

Ethan, a talented artist, had lost confidence in his abilities due to fear of scarcity. He decided to embark on a quest to overcome his self-doubt by affirming abundance. Each day, he stood in front of his studio mirror and recited powerful affirmations such as, "I am a vessel of creative abundance" and "Opportunities flow effortlessly into my life." As Ethan repeated these affirmations, a subtle shift began within him, igniting a newfound belief in his artistic prowess.

Meanwhile, Lily, a compassionate soul with a heart for service, had been feeling disconnected from her purpose. Seeking guidance, she started a gratitude journal to shift her focus from scarcity to abundance. Every evening, she poured her thoughts onto the pages, expressing gratitude for the smallest of joys, acts of kindness, and personal growth. The more Lily documented her blessings, the more her perspective expanded, and her heart became a vessel of appreciation.

As fate would have it, Ethan and Lily's paths converged during a local art exhibition. Drawn to Ethan's captivating artwork, Lily approached him with sincere admiration. A spark ignited between them, and they soon realised they shared a common desire to transcend scarcity and embrace abundance in all its forms.

With their newfound connection, Ethan and Lily embarked on a journey of exploration, supporting each other in their pursuit of abundance. They decided to combine their practices and engage in acts of generosity together, amplifying the impact of their efforts.

One day, while wandering through the city streets, they came across a struggling community centre. Inspired by their shared abundance mindset, they decided to organise an art workshop for the children in need. Ethan shared his artistic talents, guiding the children in creating vibrant paintings, while Lily showered them with encouragement and heartfelt words of appreciation.

Unexpectedly, as they immersed themselves in the workshop, a twist unfolded. Ethan, usually hesitant to share his work, was captivated by a child's doodle—a simple sketch that embodied a sense of joy and innocence. The child's untamed creativity reminded Ethan of the true essence of art, inspiring him to embrace a more spontaneous and free-spirited approach to his own creations.

Simultaneously, Lily found herself moved by the words of a young girl who expressed gratitude for the workshop, noting how it had sparked a newfound confidence within her. This unexpected twist deepened Lily's conviction to continue her acts of generosity, realising that her words and presence could profoundly impact the lives of others.

As Ethan and Lily continued their journey, their relationship blossomed, rooted in shared values of abundance and service. Together, they thrived in their practices of abundance affirmations, gratitude journaling, and acts of generosity. Each day, they discovered new dimensions of abundance, not only in material resources but also in love, creativity, and meaningful connections.

Their story became an inspiration to others in Prosperia, as the transformative power of embracing abundance rippled through the community. Through their experiences, Ethan and Lily shattered the shackles of scarcity thinking, unlocking a world of endless possibilities and fulfilment.

And so, dear reader, may the tale of Ethan and Lily remind you that by affirming abundance, cultivating gratitude, and engaging in acts of generosity, you, too, can step into a life overflowing with abundance. Embrace the unexpected twists and turns, for they hold the keys to your own personal growth and the realisation that abundance knows no bounds.

PART 3
CONTRIBUTING AND CONTENT

Welcome to Part 3 of our extraordinary journey—Contributing and Content. In this chapter, we will delve into the profound power of contribution and the immeasurable joy that comes from making a positive impact on others and the world around you.

Prepare to embark on a path that leads you to the discovery of your unique gifts and talents—a journey where the act of giving becomes an endless source of fulfilment and contentment. As we explore the power of contribution, we will unlock the secrets of finding purpose in service, understanding how aligning your work with a greater cause can bring deep meaning and satisfaction to your life.

But it doesn't stop there. In our exploration, we will also shine a light on the importance of nurturing relationships—building connections that go beyond surface-level interactions. Authentic, meaningful relationships have the power to nourish your soul, fostering a sense of belonging and contributing to your overall well-being.

Get ready to embark on a joyous adventure where you will discover the magic that lies within you and how your unique contributions can make a positive ripple effect in the lives of others. Together, we will unlock the secrets to living a life of purpose, contentment, and deep fulfilment.

So, my dear adventurer, let us step into Part 3 with open hearts and minds, ready to embrace the transformative power of contribution. Prepare to be inspired, uplifted, and motivated as we uncover the wonders that await us on this magnificent path of making a difference, finding purpose, and nurturing authentic connections. Get ready to ignite your passion for contribution and embrace the true contentment that comes from living a life of service. The journey awaits, and it's going to be nothing short of extraordinary!

CHAPTER 9
THE POWER OF CONTRIBUTION

Within each of us lies a boundless wellspring of potential—a capacity to make a positive impact on others and the world around us. When we tap into this power of contribution, we unlock a profound sense of joy, fulfilment, and purpose that surpasses personal achievements. The act of giving becomes an expression of our true essence, a testament to the interconnectedness of humanity, and a beacon of light in a world that craves compassion and kindness.

To discover the immense joy and fulfilment that comes from making a positive impact, let us embark on a journey of exploration. Here are three fun and unconventional exercises that will ignite your imagination and allow your unique contributions to shine:

1. Ripple Effect Letters:

Imagine the power of a heartfelt letter that uplifts, encourages, or expresses gratitude to someone who has made a positive impact in your life. But let's take it a step further. In this exercise, write a series of "Ripple Effect Letters" to people you may not know personally but who have influenced your life in some way. It could be an author, an artist, a teacher, or even a historical figure. Share how their work or their words have touched your heart and created a ripple effect in your own life. Send these letters out into the world, whether physically or digitally, and let the magic of your gratitude inspire others.

Dear ****

I hope this letter finds its way to you, carrying with it a deep sense of gratitude and admiration. Although we may be strangers in the traditional sense, your impact on my life has been nothing short of extraordinary. Your work, your words, and your unwavering dedication have created a ripple effect that has touched my heart and transformed my perspective.

I discovered your poetry at a time when I was feeling lost and uncertain about my own path. As I delved into its pages, I was captivated by the wisdom, insights, and the sheer authenticity that emanated from your words. Your poetic words transported me to worlds I had never imagined, but more than that, it awakened something within me—an undeniable spark of inspiration.

Your words became a guiding light, illuminating the possibilities that lie dormant within me. Through your poems, I learned the power of resilience, the beauty of embracing vulnerability, and the importance of staying true to oneself. Your insights became my companions, teaching me profound life lessons that transcended the boundaries of normality.

Since discovering your poems, I have undergone a remarkable transformation. Your words ignited a passion within me, driving me to pursue my own creative endeavours with renewed fervour. Your ability to capture the essence of the human experience, to express the rawness of emotion and the complexity of life, has shaped my own artistic journey.

Beyond my personal growth, your influence has created a ripple effect that extends beyond the confines of my own life. Your work has inspired me to share my own stories, to create art that touches the souls of others. Through my writing, I have connected with readers who have felt seen, understood, and inspired to embrace their own journeys. Your impact, my dear poet, has extended far beyond your own words, as your wisdom has transcended time and space, reaching hearts and minds around the world.

So, with profound gratitude and appreciation, I write this letter to express my heartfelt thanks. Your dedication to your craft and your willingness to share your wisdom have had an immeasurable impact on my life. You have guided me to embrace my own voice, to recognise the power of poetry, and to cherish the art of creating connections through words.

As I send this letter out into the world, I hope it serves as a ripple of gratitude, as a testament to the profound impact of your work. May it inspire you to continue sharing your gifts with the world, for there are countless souls who need the light you bring.

With heartfelt gratitude,

    A. Lovely

2. Random Acts of Creativity:

Tap into your creative spirit and engage in random acts of creativity that bring joy and inspiration to others. It could be leaving behind uplifting notes in public spaces, creating colourful sidewalk chalk art, or surprising someone with a handcrafted gift that captures their unique essence. Let your imagination run wild and infuse your surroundings with bursts of creativity and positivity. These small acts of kindness can spark a chain reaction, igniting joy in the hearts of those who encounter them.

3. Skill Swap Gatherings:

Organise a skill swap gathering within your community or circle of friends. Encourage individuals to bring their unique talents, whether it's baking, gardening, painting, playing a musical instrument, or anything else they are passionate about. During the gathering, create a joyful atmosphere where everyone can share their skills and knowledge, offering mini-lessons or demonstrations. This exchange of expertise not only fosters a sense of connection but also empowers each individual to contribute their unique gifts, creating an atmosphere of growth and collaboration.

Once upon a time, in the charming town of Serendipia, lived two individuals named Oliver and Emma. Oliver was an excellent baker, known for his mouth-watering pastries, while Emma possessed a remarkable talent for painting vibrant and captivating artwork. Unbeknownst to them, their paths were about to intersect in the most delightful way.

One sunny day, Oliver was strolling through the park when he noticed an elderly woman, Mrs. Jenkins, struggling with her grocery bags. Without hesitation, Oliver rushed to her side, offering a helping hand. Together, they managed to gather the bags, and Oliver insisted on escorting Mrs. Jenkins back to her home. During their walk, Mrs. Jenkins shared stories of her younger days, and Oliver listened attentively, soaking in her wisdom and warmth.

In gratitude, Mrs. Jenkins invited Oliver to her humble abode, where she shared a treasured family recipe for a delectable apple pie. Oliver, overwhelmed by her generosity, promised to bake the pie, and deliver it to her the following day. Little did he know that this simple act of kindness would set a beautiful chain of events into motion.

Meanwhile, Emma was seeking a way to showcase her artwork and connect with the community. She stumbled upon an invitation for a Skill Swap Gathering, organised by a local community centre. Excitement coursed through her as she realised this would be the perfect opportunity to share her passion for painting while embracing new experiences.

On the day of the gathering, Oliver arrived with his freshly baked apple pie, eager to swap his baking skills for something equally enchanting. Emma, adorned with a vibrant painting she had carefully selected, entered the room, her heart brimming with anticipation. The air buzzed with excitement as the attendees exchanged their skills and knowledge, creating an atmosphere of learning and camaraderie.

Emma caught sight of Mrs. Jenkins, who had also attended the gathering. She couldn't resist the urge to capture Mrs. Jenkins' radiant spirit on canvas. Emma approached her and kindly asked if she could paint her portrait. Overwhelmed by the request, Mrs. Jenkins hesitantly agreed, unaware of the profound impact this simple gesture would have.

As Emma worked on the portrait, she engaged in heartfelt conversations with Mrs. Jenkins, learning about her life experiences, dreams, and aspirations. In turn, Mrs. Jenkins marvelled at Emma's talent, feeling deeply honoured to be the subject of her artwork. Their connection grew, bridging generational gaps and fostering a friendship that transcended time.

Meanwhile, Oliver found himself sharing baking secrets and techniques with a young aspiring chef, Jacob. The exchange of knowledge and passion fuelled their enthusiasm, igniting a flame of creativity within both of them. Inspired by Jacob's innovative ideas, Oliver discovered new ways to infuse his pastries with unique flavours and designs, pushing the boundaries of his culinary expertise.

As the gathering came to an end, Oliver presented Mrs. Jenkins with the freshly baked apple pie he had promised. Overwhelmed with gratitude, she savoured each bite, cherishing the flavours and the memories it evoked. Emma, too, gifted Mrs. Jenkins with a framed portrait, capturing her vibrant spirit and illuminating the love and respect they had developed for one another.

In the weeks that followed, the effects of their random act of kindness and the skill swap gathering began to unfold. Mrs. Jenkins shared her apple pie with her neighbours, spreading warmth and joy throughout the community. Emma's portrait of Mrs. Jenkins became a symbol of love and connection, reminding everyone of the beauty in embracing intergenerational friendships.

Oliver, inspired by Jacob's innovative ideas, began experimenting with new pastry recipes, creating a line of desserts that caught the attention of a local café. His delectable treats became a source of delight and celebration, attracting customers from far and wide.

As for Emma, her portrait of Mrs. Jenkins was showcased in a community art exhibition. It touched the hearts of many, evoking a sense of nostalgia and reminding them of the power of human connection. Her art became a catalyst for conversations, opening doors to new friendships and collaborations within the community.

And so, the ripple effect of Oliver and Emma's random acts of kindness and their participation in the skill swap gathering continued to spread, uplifting spirits, and creating a tapestry of joy and connection in Serendipia. It served as a reminder that when we share our talents, kindness, and creativity with others, the impact we make can surpass our wildest dreams.

In the end, Oliver and Emma discovered that through their acts of kindness and their willingness to share their gifts, they not only transformed the lives of others but also found fulfilment and purpose in their own journey. And as they continued to embrace the power of contribution, their lives became a testament to the profound and lasting effects of genuine connection, generosity, and the magic that occurs when we come together in the spirit of sharing.

These exercises go beyond the conventional notions of contribution, encouraging you to think outside the box and unleash your creative spirit. As you embark on these adventures, you will witness the transformative power of your contributions, both in the lives of others and within yourself. The joy and fulfilment that come from making a positive impact are boundless, creating a ripple effect that extends far beyond what we can imagine.

So, my fellow adventurer, embrace the power of contribution and step into the realm of joy, fulfilment, and purpose. Let your unique contributions shine, igniting a wave of positive change that spreads throughout the world. Through these unconventional exercises, you will uncover the true essence of contribution and discover the immeasurable beauty that comes from uplifting others. The power is within you, waiting to be unleashed. Embrace it, and watch as your contributions become beacons of light, illuminating the path for others to follow.

CHAPTER 10
FINDING PURPOSE IN SERVICE

Amidst the tapestry of life, there lies a profound secret to unlocking deep contentment and a profound sense of fulfilment—finding purpose in service. When we align our work with a greater purpose, when we embrace the call to make a difference in the lives of others and the world around us, we discover a path that leads to boundless joy and a profound sense of fulfilment.

In this chapter, we embark on a soul-stirring exploration of finding purpose in service. We delve into the transformative power of aligning our work with a greater cause—a purpose that goes beyond personal success and taps into the collective tapestry of humanity. It is a journey that invites us to listen to the whispers of our hearts, to embrace the unique gifts we possess, and to step into the world as catalysts of positive change.

Finding purpose in service invites us to look beyond the boundaries of our own desires and to gaze upon the needs of others. It is an invitation to lift others up, to lend a helping hand, and to contribute to the betterment of our communities and the world at large. It is through acts of service, both big and small, that we cultivate a deep sense of meaning and fulfilment that cannot be attained through personal accomplishments alone.

As we embark on this exploration, we will encounter stories of individuals who have discovered their purpose through service—a teacher who ignites the flame of learning in young minds, a social entrepreneur who empowers marginalised communities, or a volunteer who brings hope to those in need. Their journeys will inspire us to uncover our own unique path and recognise the myriad ways in which our skills, passions, and experiences can be channelled to make a positive impact.

Through reflection, introspection, and heartfelt exploration, we will uncover the seeds of purpose that lie within us, waiting to bloom into something magnificent. We will delve into the interconnectedness of our lives, recognising that our purpose is intricately woven into the fabric of the world—a tapestry where every thread, every action, every moment of service contributes to a greater whole.

So, my fellow seeker of purpose, prepare to embark on a voyage of self-discovery and service. Open your heart to the possibilities that lie ahead, for within them lies the key to deep contentment and a profound sense of fulfilment. As we explore the depths of finding purpose in service, may we awaken to the truth that our greatest fulfilment comes not from what we receive, but from what we give. Together, let us illuminate the world with our unique contributions, weaving a tapestry of love, compassion, and lasting change.

Here are three fun and exercises to help you delve into service and explore how aligning your work with a greater purpose can lead to deep contentment and a sense of fulfilment:

1. Kindness Scavenger Hunt:

Embark on a kindness scavenger hunt where you actively seek out opportunities to perform random acts of kindness throughout your day. Create a list of kind actions, such as buying a coffee for a stranger, leaving uplifting notes in public spaces, or offering assistance to someone in need. As you go about your day, check off the acts of kindness you complete and reflect on how they made you and the recipients feel. Notice the ripple effect of your actions and how aligning your work with the purpose of spreading kindness brings a deep sense of fulfilment.

2. Skills for Service Swap:

Gather a group of friends, family members, or colleagues and organise a Skills for Service Swap event. Each person can offer their unique skills and talents to others in exchange for a service they need. For example, if you're a web designer, you can offer to create a website for someone in exchange for a cooking lesson from a skilled chef. This exercise allows you to explore the concept of service beyond traditional volunteer work, tapping into the diverse talents within your community and fostering meaningful connections. Reflect on how aligning your skills with the purpose of serving others brings a sense of fulfilment and deepens your connection with those around you.

3. Serendipitous Acts of Service:

Embrace serendipity by engaging in acts of service that arise spontaneously throughout your day. Rather than planning specific acts, stay open to the opportunities that present themselves. It could be helping someone struggling with their groceries, offering a listening ear to a friend in need, or volunteering your time at a local community centre. Notice how these serendipitous acts of service align with your purpose and bring a sense of contentment and fulfilment. Reflect on the interconnectedness of these experiences and how they contribute to the greater tapestry of service in the world.

These exercises provide unique and playful ways to explore service, allowing you to go beyond the conventional approaches and tap into the joy and fulfilment that comes from aligning your work with a greater purpose. Embrace the spirit of adventure, open your heart to the unexpected, and let the magic of service lead you on a path of deep contentment and purposeful living.

A couple of fun short stories to inspire...

Once upon a time, in the enchanting village of Heart-warming Haven, lived two remarkable individuals named Maya and Ben. Maya was an enthusiastic gardener, while Ben possessed a natural talent for storytelling. Little did they know that their shared passion for service and aligning their work with a greater purpose would lead them on a whimsical adventure of deep contentment and fulfilment.

One sunny day, Maya was tending to her vibrant garden when she noticed a sign in the village square. It read, "Calling all storytellers! Share your tales with those who need a spark of joy." Intrigued, she followed the sign and arrived at a small gathering under a grand oak tree. There, she met Ben, a charismatic storyteller who had organised the event.

Curiosity sparked, Maya approached Ben and shared her desire to contribute to the community through her love for gardening. Ben's eyes gleamed with excitement as an idea sprouted in his mind. He proposed a collaborative project where they would create a storytelling garden—a magical place where stories would come alive amidst nature's beauty.

Eager to embark on this endeavour, Maya and Ben gathered a group of villagers who shared their passion for service. Together, they transformed an unused piece of land into a whimsical garden, filled with flowers, winding paths, and cosy reading nooks. Each plant in the garden held a story, waiting to be discovered.

As the storytelling garden flourished, Maya's gardening skills and Ben's storytelling talent intertwined in a symphony of creativity and service. Maya planted flowers that corresponded to the characters in Ben's stories, creating a sensory experience where visitors could immerse themselves in tales that came to life through nature's touch.

Word of the storytelling garden spread far and wide, attracting visitors from neighbouring villages. Children laughed as they listened to Ben's animated stories while exploring the enchanting garden. Adults found solace in the garden's serene corners, discovering new perspectives through the tales they encountered.

One day, as Maya tended to the garden, she noticed a young boy named Oliver sitting alone on a bench, his eyes filled with sadness. Curiosity sparked, she approached him and gently asked if he would like to share his story. Oliver's face lit up with a mixture of surprise and longing. He poured out his heart, sharing his dreams and fears with Maya.

Moved by his vulnerability, Maya invited Oliver to join their storytelling garden project. With the guidance of Ben's stories, Maya nurtured Oliver's budding interest in gardening, teaching him the art of cultivating beauty from the earth. As Oliver immersed himself in the garden, he discovered a sense of purpose and belonging, transforming his sadness into a spark of joy.

The storytelling garden continued to grow, drawing people from all walks of life. Maya, Ben, and Oliver revelled in the connections they formed and the stories they shared. They witnessed the transformative power of aligning their work with a greater purpose—to bring joy, inspiration, and a sense of belonging to those who sought solace within the garden's embrace.

As time passed, the storytelling garden became a haven for both locals and travellers alike. Its lush beauty and captivating tales infused the hearts of all who wandered its paths. Maya, Ben, and Oliver discovered that in serving others and aligning their work with a greater purpose, they experienced a profound sense of contentment and fulfilment that radiated from their souls.

And so, in the heart of Heart-warming Haven, the storytelling garden flourished, serving as a testament to the magic that occurs when individuals embrace service and align their work with a greater purpose. Maya, Ben, and Oliver continued to nurture the garden and share their gifts, creating a ripple effect of joy and fulfilment that touched the lives of countless souls.

In the end, they realised that true contentment lies not in personal achievements alone, but in the profound impact they made through service—to create spaces of enchantment, ignite the spark of imagination, and nurture the souls of those seeking connection and inspiration. Their journey taught them that in the tapestry of service, they found their true purpose and a sense of fulfilment that would forever bloom within their hearts.

And.. here's a heart-warming tale about teaching and service:

In the bustling town of Brightville, there lived a passionate teacher named Ms. Harper. She possessed an innate ability to inspire young minds, igniting their curiosity and nurturing their thirst for knowledge. Ms. Harper understood the power of aligning her work with a greater purpose—a purpose that went beyond academic achievement and touched the very core of her students' lives.

Each morning, as Ms. Harper entered her colourful classroom, she would feel a sense of anticipation in the air. The walls were adorned with vibrant artwork, showcasing her students' creativity. The desks were arranged in a way that encouraged collaboration and connection. But it was the joy in her students' eyes that truly reflected the impact of her purposeful teaching.

Ms. Harper believed that education was not solely about textbooks and exams; it was about shaping young minds and nurturing the whole child. She designed her lessons to inspire critical thinking, empathy, and a deep sense of compassion. She encouraged her students to explore their passions, to ask questions, and to make a positive difference in the world.

One day, Ms. Harper received an invitation to a national teaching conference. Eager to expand her own knowledge and share her insights, she embarked on a journey to a bustling city where educators from far and wide gathered to exchange ideas. Little did she know that this experience would profoundly shape her understanding of service and deepen her sense of purpose.

At the conference, Ms. Harper met a teacher named Mr. Sullivan, who hailed from a remote village nestled in the mountains. Mr. Sullivan had devoted his life to educating children in underprivileged communities, where access to quality education was limited. His commitment to service and his unwavering dedication moved Ms. Harper deeply.

As they conversed, Mr. Sullivan shared stories of his students' resilience, their thirst for knowledge despite their challenging circumstances. Inspired by his words, Ms. Harper realised that her purpose as a teacher extended beyond the walls of her classroom. She felt a calling to serve those in need and make a difference in the lives of students who lacked access to quality education.

Upon her return to Brightville, Ms. Harper gathered her students and shared her newfound insights with them. She proposed a project that would involve partnering with Mr. Sullivan's school and supporting the education of children in underprivileged communities. The students' eyes lit up with excitement, eager to embrace the spirit of service and contribute to a cause greater than themselves.

Together, Ms. Harper's class and Mr. Sullivan's students embarked on a journey of collaboration and learning. They organised fundraisers, book drives, and pen pal exchanges, bridging the gap between their two worlds. The students discovered the profound impact of aligning their education with a purpose—to empower others, to share knowledge, and to create opportunities for those less fortunate.

As the project unfolded, the students experienced a deep sense of fulfilment and contentment. They witnessed first-hand the transformative power of education and service. Their empathy grew, and they developed a profound understanding of the world beyond their own. The joy of making a positive difference in the lives of others became a guiding force in their own personal journeys.

Years passed, and Ms. Harper's students continued to embrace service in their lives. They pursued careers that aligned with their passions and allowed them to make a positive impact on society. Some became teachers, carrying the torch of purposeful education forward. Others entered fields of social work, medicine, and advocacy, spreading kindness and knowledge wherever they went.

As for Ms. Harper, she found deep contentment and fulfilment in the knowledge that her teaching had extended far beyond the confines of her classroom. The seeds of service she had planted in her students had blossomed into a beautiful tapestry of compassion and change. She knew that she had found her purpose in aligning her work with a greater cause, and the ripple effect of her efforts would continue to touch lives for generations to come.

In the end, the story of Ms. Harper and her students serves as a reminder that when we align our work with a greater purpose, when we serve others through our passions and talents, we unlock a profound sense of fulfilment and contentment. The impact we make in the lives of others becomes the true measure of our success, shaping not only their journeys but our own as well. And in the tapestry of teaching and service, we find the power to transform lives and create a brighter, more compassionate world.

CHAPTER 11
NURTURING RELATIONSHIPS

In the intricate tapestry of life, one thread stands out as particularly vital—the thread of relationships. Nurturing authentic connections and fostering meaningful relationships is a cornerstone of our well-being and contributes to a profound sense of fulfilment and joy. It is through these bonds that we find solace, support, and a deep sense of belonging.

In this chapter, we embark on a heartfelt exploration of the importance of nurturing relationships. We delve into the beauty of authentic connections—the friendships that weather the storms of life, the family ties that anchor us in love, and the serendipitous encounters that forever change our paths. We will uncover the profound impact these relationships have on our overall well-being and how they contribute to the richness and depth of our lives.

Recognising the importance of nurturing relationships invites us to embrace vulnerability, to open our hearts to the possibility of deep connection, and to cultivate a genuine presence in the lives of others. It is a reminder that we are not meant to navigate this journey alone, but to weave our stories together, supporting and uplifting one another along the way.

Throughout this chapter, we will delve into the transformative power of meaningful relationships. We will explore the practices that nurture and sustain these bonds—active listening, empathetic communication, and acts of kindness. We will discover how nurturing relationships not only brings joy and fulfilment to our own lives but also serves as a catalyst for positive change in the lives of those we encounter.

We will encounter stories of individuals whose lives have been forever touched by the power of authentic connections—a stranger offering a helping hand, a friend lending an empathetic ear, or a mentor guiding someone on their path. These stories will inspire us to recognise the profound impact we can make through nurturing relationships and to cherish the connections we hold dear.

As we venture further into the exploration of nurturing relationships, let us approach this chapter with open hearts and a willingness to deepen our understanding of the human experience. Let us recognise that in cultivating authentic connections, we not only enrich our own lives but also contribute to the collective tapestry of humanity, creating a world where compassion, love, and understanding thrive.

So, my fellow seeker of meaningful connections, prepare to embark on a journey that will illuminate the beauty and importance of nurturing relationships. Let us honour the bonds that grace our lives and embrace the power of genuine connection. Together, let us weave a tapestry of love, compassion, and profound well-being as we nurture the relationships that bring us joy and make our lives truly meaningful.

Here are three fun and lively examples to explore the importance of building authentic connections and fostering meaningful relationships:

1. The Appreciation Adventure:

Embark on an appreciation adventure where you gather a group of friends or loved ones for a day filled with gratitude and connection. Each person takes turns expressing heartfelt appreciation for someone else in the group, highlighting their unique qualities, and sharing how they have positively impacted their lives. This exercise not only deepens the bonds between individuals but also creates an atmosphere of love and appreciation that permeates the entire gathering. It's a lively and uplifting way to foster meaningful connections and celebrate the joy of authentic relationships.

2. The Serendipitous Social:

Organise a serendipitous social event where you encourage attendees to engage in spontaneous conversations with strangers. Instead of relying on small talk, encourage them to ask thought-provoking questions that foster deeper connections. For example, "What's one thing you're most proud of accomplishing?" or "What brings you the most joy in life?" By encouraging genuine and meaningful conversations, this exercise opens the door for authentic connections to blossom and reminds participants of the beauty of human connection in unexpected places.

3. The Relationship Recipe Swap:

Host a relationship recipe swap, where friends and family members come together to share their "recipes" for successful relationships. Each person brings a handwritten note or a small booklet containing their unique insights and advice for nurturing connections. The recipes could include ingredients such as open communication, acts of kindness, shared experiences, and heartfelt gestures. This lively exchange sparks engaging conversations and provides a treasure trove of wisdom for building and nurturing meaningful relationships. Participants leave with a collection of heartfelt recipes that serve as a reminder of the importance of authentic connections in their lives.

These lively and unconventional exercises offer opportunities to explore the importance of building authentic connections and fostering meaningful relationships in fun and engaging ways. They encourage participants to dive deeper, celebrate one another, and embrace the beauty of human connection. So, gather your loved ones, embark on these adventures, and let the joy of authentic relationships fill your lives with laughter, love, and profound well-being.

Here are some facts on the importance of building authentic connections and fostering meaningful relationships:

1. Enhanced Well-being: Numerous studies have shown that having strong and meaningful relationships contributes to overall well-being. People with close connections tend to experience lower levels of stress, anxiety, and depression. They also report higher levels of life satisfaction and happiness.

2. Longer Lifespan: Research has found that individuals with strong social connections tend to live longer lives. Studies show that those who have strong relationships and social support systems have a reduced risk of mortality compared to those who are socially isolated.

3. Mental and Emotional Resilience: Authentic connections play a crucial role in developing mental and emotional resilience. Having a support system of trusted individuals who can provide comfort, advice, and understanding during challenging times can help individuals navigate difficulties more effectively and bounce back from setbacks.

4. Increased Self-Esteem: Meaningful relationships can contribute to higher self-esteem and a positive self-image. When we feel accepted, valued, and loved by others, it boosts our confidence and helps us develop a more positive perception of ourselves.

5. Stress Reduction: Building authentic connections and fostering meaningful relationships can help reduce stress levels. When we have someone to share our burdens with or seek emotional support from, it can alleviate stress and provide a sense of comfort and relief.

6. Personal Growth: Meaningful relationships provide opportunities for personal growth and self-discovery. Interacting with others who have different perspectives and experiences broadens our understanding of the world and helps us develop empathy, compassion, and a greater sense of openness.

7. Support and Encouragement: Authentic connections offer a support network that provides encouragement, motivation, and accountability. Having people who believe in us and cheer us on can inspire us to pursue our goals, overcome challenges, and reach our full potential.

8. Increased Happiness: Meaningful relationships contribute to overall happiness and life satisfaction. Studies have consistently shown that people with strong social connections report higher levels of happiness and well-being compared to those who feel socially isolated.

9. Improved Physical Health: Building authentic connections has been linked to improved physical health outcomes. Research suggests that individuals with strong relationships may have a lower risk of developing chronic

illnesses, such as cardiovascular diseases, and may experience faster recovery times from illnesses and surgeries.

10. Sense of Belonging: Meaningful relationships create a sense of belonging and connectedness. When we feel connected to others, we feel a part of something greater than ourselves, fostering a sense of purpose, identity, and community.

These facts highlight the profound impact that building authentic connections and fostering meaningful relationships can have on our well-being, happiness, and overall quality of life. Investing in these connections not only enriches our own lives but also creates a ripple effect of positivity and support in the lives of those around us.

PART 4
PURPOSE WITH PEACE

In the realm of purpose, a serene path awaits, where the yearning for meaning converges with the pursuit of peace. Part 4: Purpose with Peace invites you to embark on a soulful journey of self-discovery, as you navigate the intricate dance between clarity of purpose and the tranquillity of inner harmony.

Within these pages, we delve into the art of clarifying your purpose, peering deep into the recesses of your being to uncover the whispers of your soul. Through reflection and introspection, we unravel the threads that weave together your passions, values, and unique gifts, shedding light on how they intersect with your professional endeavours. As you gain clarity, a profound sense of purpose emerges, guiding your steps towards a life that is aligned with your authentic self.

But the journey towards purpose is not without its challenges. We explore the delicate balance between ambition and inner peace—a dance that requires grace, resilience, and self-awareness. It is a call to cultivate inner tranquillity even amidst the pursuit of external success, recognising that true fulfilment lies not only in achieving goals but in maintaining a harmonious state of being along the way.

Mindfulness and self-care become our trusted companions on this transformative expedition. We delve into the art of mindfulness, embracing the power of presence and deep awareness in every moment. We discover the profound impact of self-care—nurturing our bodies, minds, and spirits with kindness and compassion. Through these practices, we weave a tapestry of well-being, sustaining our sense of peace as we navigate the ebb and flow of life's currents.

In this chapter, we honour the delicate dance between purpose and peace, understanding that our true calling extends beyond professional achievements alone. It beckons us to listen to the whispers of our hearts, to honour the gentle rhythms of our souls, and to create a life that embraces both purposeful ambition and inner serenity.

So, my fellow seeker of purpose and peace, prepare to embark on this transformative chapter, where clarity and tranquillity converge. Let us explore the depths of our being, uncover the treasures that lie within, and chart a course that aligns our purpose with the serenity of our souls. As we navigate the path of purpose with peace, may we find fulfilment, meaning, and a profound sense of contentment that illuminates our every step.

CHAPTER 12
CLARIFYING YOUR PURPOSE

In the vast tapestry of existence, our purpose awaits, eager to be discovered and embraced. Part 4: Clarifying Your Purpose invites you on a transformative journey of self-reflection, guiding you to unravel the intricacies of your life's purpose and illuminate the path that intersects with your professional endeavours. Get ready to embark on a quest that is equal parts introspection, imagination, and joyful exploration.

1. Purpose Collage:

Grab a stack of magazines, scissors, and a large poster board. Dive into the colourful pages and let your intuition guide you as you cut out images, words, and phrases that resonate with your heart. Arrange these snippets of inspiration on the poster board, creating a purpose collage that visually captures the essence of your aspirations, passions, and values. Allow your creativity to flow freely, as you delve into the depths of your subconscious and bring your purpose to life in vibrant colours and imagery.

2. Meaningful Moments Map:

Create a "Meaningful Moments Map" to trace the significant experiences and moments that have shaped your life. Take a large sheet of paper or use a digital platform and draw a winding path. Along this path, mark the pivotal moments, achievements, and encounters that hold significance to you. Reflect on the emotions, lessons, and growth that each moment brought. This playful activity not only helps you identify patterns and themes but also sheds light on the tapestry of experiences that have led you to where you are today, providing valuable clues to your purpose.

3. Purposeful Interview:

Imagine yourself as both the interviewer and the interviewee in a thought-provoking conversation about purpose. Prepare a list of questions that dive deep into your values, passions, and dreams. Sit in a quiet space, take on the role of the interviewer, and ask yourself these questions. Allow your thoughts and insights to flow freely as you respond, exploring the depths of your being and uncovering the layers that make up your purpose. This playful and introspective exercise encourages self-discovery and offers fresh perspectives on the intricacies of your purpose.

Once upon a time in a small town nestled amidst rolling hills, lived a diverse group of individuals yearning to discover the true purpose that lay within their hearts. They found themselves drawn to a gathering organised by a wise old storyteller known for her ability to illuminate the hidden depths of the human soul.

On a sunny afternoon, the townsfolk gathered in a picturesque garden, where colourful flowers bloomed, and a gentle breeze carried whispers of possibility. The storyteller welcomed them with a warm smile, her eyes twinkling with wisdom and curiosity.

The gathering commenced with an invitation to embark on a purposeful interview—a conversation that would unlock the doors to self-discovery and illuminate the path to their life's purpose. The townsfolk paired up, their faces filled with a mixture of anticipation and trepidation, as they prepared to engage in profound dialogue.

Sarah, a passionate artist with dreams of bringing beauty to the world through her creations, was paired with John, a wise and introspective philosopher. As they sat under the shade of an old oak tree, Sarah took a deep breath, ready to dive into the depths of her purpose.

John, with gentle curiosity, asked Sarah a series of thought-provoking questions: "What brings you the greatest joy in your artistic expression? How do you envision your art impacting others? What do you hope to leave as a legacy through your work?"

As Sarah pondered each question, a transformation began to unfold. Through the interview, she not only articulated her dreams and aspirations but discovered the underlying values and passions that fuelled her creative fire. The conversation ignited a profound sense of clarity and purpose within her, like a guiding light illuminating the path ahead.

Inspired by Sarah and John's deep engagement, others in the garden also delved into purposeful interviews. Conversations echoed through the air as the townsfolk shared their hopes, dreams, and aspirations with newfound clarity and conviction. Each interview became a journey of self-discovery, peeling back layers of doubt and uncertainty to reveal the radiant core of their being.

As the day unfolded, the impact of these purposeful interviews rippled through the lives of the townsfolk. Sarah, armed with a renewed sense of purpose, started pouring her heart into her art like never before. Her paintings radiated with the essence of her true self, capturing the beauty she saw in the world and inspiring others to see it too.

Others found the courage to pursue their long-held dreams, whether it was starting a non-profit organisation, writing a book, or dedicating themselves to a cause close to their hearts. The purposeful interviews had not only awakened their individual passions but also ignited a collective fire of purpose within the community.

Over time, the once-sleepy town transformed into a vibrant hub of purpose-driven individuals, each contributing their unique gifts to create a more beautiful and meaningful world. The ripple effect of those purposeful interviews continued to expand, touching the lives of countless others far beyond the confines of their small town.

And so, in the garden where purposeful interviews began, the townsfolk discovered that the profound impact of these conversations was not limited to their own lives. Through the power of self-reflection and meaningful dialogue, they unleashed the boundless potential within them, creating a tapestry of purpose, joy, and inspiration that forever changed the course of their lives and the world around them.

From that day forward, purposeful interviews became a treasured tradition in the town, a reminder of the transformative power that lies within each individual and the profound effect that a simple conversation can have on the course of one's life. And as the storyteller watched the town flourish with purpose, she knew that the seeds of purposeful interviews had sown a garden of transformation, blossoming with lives aligned with their true calling.

A fun and lively example of the effect of a Meaningful Moments Map:

In the bustling city of Brightville, a group of friends decided to embark on a creative adventure to explore their meaningful moments and discover the hidden gems that shaped their lives. They gathered in a vibrant café, armed with colourful markers, a large sheet of paper, and their boundless curiosity.

As they sipped on their favourite beverages and savoured delectable treats, the friends spread the paper on the table and drew a winding path—a whimsical journey that would trace the significant moments that held a special place in their hearts.

With laughter and excitement filling the air, they took turns sharing their meaningful moments and placing markers along the path to mark each significant experience. The moments were as diverse as the friends themselves—some marked academic achievements, others marked personal milestones, and a few marked serendipitous encounters that forever altered their trajectories.

As they created their Meaningful Moments Map, something magical began to unfold. Memories flooded back, and emotions sparked a sense of nostalgia and appreciation. They laughed, they cried, and they celebrated the collective tapestry of experiences that shaped their unique journeys.

Amy, a spirited dancer, marked the moment she had her first solo performance. She recalled the electrifying energy that coursed through her veins as she glided across the stage, igniting her passion for dance.

Tom, a passionate traveller, marked the moment he stood in awe at the majestic Grand Canyon. The vastness of the canyon reminded him of the limitless possibilities that life holds, fuelling his thirst for exploration and adventure.

Emily, a compassionate volunteer, marked the moment she helped build a school in a remote village. The joy and gratitude on the children's faces sparked a fire within her to continue making a positive impact on the lives of others.

As they shared their stories and moved along the path, they discovered common threads and shared experiences, deepening their bond as friends. The Meaningful Moments Map became a tapestry of interconnected stories, a testament to the power of shared experiences and the beauty of their friendships.

In the weeks that followed, the friends displayed their Meaningful Moments Maps in their homes. It became a source of inspiration—a visual reminder of the richness and depth of their lives, even during challenging times.

The maps also served as a catalyst for future adventures. They planned trips to revisit meaningful locations, rekindle old passions, and create new memories together. The Meaningful Moments Map had unlocked a treasure trove of possibilities, urging them to embrace each moment with gratitude and intention.

Over time, the friends realised that their Meaningful Moments Map had become more than just a vibrant collage of memories—it had become a testament to their resilience, growth, and shared humanity. It reminded them to cherish every moment, celebrate their individual and collective journeys, and embrace the beauty of being present.

And so, as they continued to add markers along their winding path of life, the friends discovered that their Meaningful Moments Map was not just a snapshot of the past but a compass guiding them toward a future filled with purpose, joy, and a deep appreciation for the meaningful moments yet to come.

These three creative activities invite you to embark on a journey of self-reflection, embracing a sense of wonder and curiosity as you navigate the path to clarifying your purpose. Through collages, maps, and purposeful interviews, you engage your imagination, tap into your intuition, and uncover the treasures that lie within. Remember, this journey is unique to you, and as you explore, allow your heart to guide you, illuminating the path where your life's purpose intertwines with your professional endeavours. Embrace the joy of self-discovery and let your purpose unfold, like a magnificent tapestry, revealing the true essence of who you are and the meaningful contributions you are destined to make in the world.

CHAPTER 13
BALANCING AMBITION AND INNER PEACE

In the dance of life, ambition, and inner peace twirl hand in hand, creating a harmonious rhythm that propels us towards success while nurturing our soul. Part 4: Balancing Ambition and Inner Peace invites you to embark on a transformative journey where you cultivate inner tranquillity, embrace ambition, and create a sustainable approach to success that nourishes both your aspirations and your well-being.

Within these pages, we explore the delicate art of balancing ambition and inner peace, recognising that true success lies not only in the external achievements but also in the state of inner contentment that accompanies our journey. As you embark on this path, you'll discover that cultivating inner peace is the cornerstone of sustainable success, empowering you to navigate challenges with grace, maintain a sense of balance, and live in alignment with your authentic self.

To guide you on this journey, we have curated three empowering exercises, each designed to nourish different aspects of your being:

Harmonious Meditation:

Find a quiet space, take a comfortable seat, and close your eyes. Allow your breath to steady as you dive into a meditation practice focused on cultivating inner peace and harmony. Visualise a serene garden within your mind's eye, filled with lush greenery and vibrant flowers. With each inhale, imagine breathing in tranquillity, and with each exhale, release any tension or stress. As you continue this meditation, allow a sense of inner calm to wash over you, nurturing your soul and restoring balance to your being.

Breathwork for Ambition:

Sit in a comfortable position, taking a moment to ground yourself. With focused intention, engage in a breathwork practice that ignites your ambition and fuels your drive. Take a deep inhale, allowing your breath to expand and fill your lungs. Exhale fully, releasing any self-doubt or limitations. As you continue this rhythmic breathing, visualise yourself stepping into the arena of your ambitions, feeling a surge of confidence and determination. With each breath, inhale the energy of possibility and exhale any resistance, embracing your innate potential and aligning it with your ambitious pursuits.

Joyful Creativity:

Tap into your inner child and let your imagination run wild with a fun and creative activity of your choosing. It could be painting, dancing, singing, or any form of self-expression that brings you joy. Embrace this moment of playfulness and allow your creativity to flow freely. As you engage in this activity, release any expectations or judgments, and simply revel in the pure delight of creation.

Sustaining Inner Peace: Joyful Expression

Embrace a playful and fun activity that brings you immense joy and helps sustain your inner peace. It could be dancing freely to your favourite music, painting with vibrant colours, or immersing yourself in nature. Engage in this joyful expression regularly, allowing it to rejuvenate your spirit and provide a respite from the demands of your ambitions. Let the sheer joy of the activity remind you of the importance of nurturing your well-being and maintaining a balanced approach to success.

As you embrace these exercises, remember that balancing ambition and inner peace is not a one-time endeavour but a lifelong practice. It requires self-awareness, adaptability, and a willingness to listen to the whispers of your heart. By cultivating inner peace, igniting ambition, and sustaining the delicate equilibrium between the two, you create a foundation for a balanced and fulfilling journey towards success.

So, my ambitious soul, prepare to embark on this transformative work where ambition and inner peace harmonise. Allow the practices of cultivating inner peace, igniting ambition, and sustaining well-being to guide you on your path. With each mindful breath, each joyful expression, and each moment of inner serenity, you align your ambitious aspirations with the steady rhythm of your heart, creating a sustainable approach to success that embraces both achievement and tranquillity. Embrace the dance, find your balance, and let your journey unfold with grace, purpose, and an abiding sense of inner peace.

And... here is an example of finding balance with ambition and peace:

In the bustling city of Harmonyville, a man named Alex and a woman named Maya found themselves on separate paths towards cultivating inner peace while pursuing their ambitious goals. Though their journeys were unique, they both sought the delicate balance that would allow them to thrive without sacrificing their inner tranquillity.

Alex was a driven entrepreneur with a passion for innovation. He was determined to build a successful tech start-up and make a lasting impact in the industry. However, he often found himself overwhelmed by the demands of his work, causing his inner peace to waver.

Recognising the importance of balance, Alex embarked on a quest to cultivate inner peace. He began incorporating mindfulness practices into his daily routine, taking short breaks throughout the day to practice deep breathing and mindful meditation. These moments of stillness helped him reconnect with his inner calm, allowing him to navigate the challenges of entrepreneurship with greater clarity and composure.

Maya, on the other hand, was a talented artist with a burning desire to share her creativity with the world. She longed to express herself authentically while maintaining a sense of inner peace. Despite her passion, she often felt torn between the pursuit of her artistic dreams and the pressures of external validation.

To find her balance, Maya turned to practices that nurtured her inner peace. She discovered the power of journaling as a means of self-expression and self-reflection. Each day, she would pour her thoughts and emotions onto the pages of her journal, allowing her innermost fears and aspirations to be witnessed and released. Through this practice, Maya gained clarity on her artistic vision and developed a resilient mindset that shielded her from external pressures.

As Alex and Maya continued their journeys towards balance, they both realised the significance of incorporating self-care practices into their lives. Alex dedicated time to engage in activities that brought him joy, such as playing his favourite musical instrument and spending quality time with loved ones. Maya, on the other hand, found solace in immersing herself in nature, taking long walks and sketching the beauty she encountered.

Over time, Alex and Maya began to witness the transformative power of cultivating inner peace while pursuing their ambitious goals. They discovered that the more they nurtured their well-being, the greater their capacity to make meaningful contributions in their respective fields. They became shining examples of how balance and sustainability could coexist with success.

Their journeys not only inspired others but also created a ripple effect in their communities. Through their actions, they demonstrated that ambition need not come at the expense of inner peace. They inspired fellow entrepreneurs, artists, and dreamers to seek harmony, reminding them that the pursuit of success is most fulfilling when coupled with a grounded sense of tranquillity.

As Alex and Maya continued their paths, they found solace in the knowledge that they were not alone. They recognised that their shared desire to cultivate inner peace while pursuing their goals connected them in a profound way. They supported one another, exchanging insights, and encouraging each other to maintain their balance, even in the face of challenges.

In their journey towards balancing ambition and inner peace, Alex and Maya discovered that success was not defined solely by external achievements but by the peace and fulfilment they felt within. They became living embodiments of the harmonious dance between ambition and serenity, inspiring others to embrace the same delicate balance as they pursued their own ambitious endeavours.

And so, in the city of Harmonyville, their stories intertwined, symbolising the infinite possibilities that arise when ambition and inner peace are aligned. Through their example, they illuminated a path that beckoned others to cultivate inner peace, foster harmony, and pursue their goals with a sustainable and balanced approach.

CHAPTER 14
MINDFULNESS AND SELF-CARE

Amidst the constant rhythm of life, there lies a sanctuary within you—a sanctuary where mindfulness, self-care, and self-compassion converge, nurturing your well-being and cradling a sense of peace. Part 4: Mindfulness and Self-Care invites you to embark on a transformative exploration of practices that foster a deep connection with the present moment, prioritise your well-being, and cultivate self-compassion as a guiding light on your journey.

In this chapter, we delve into the art of mindfulness, the essence of self-care, and the power of self-compassion as foundational pillars that nourish your mind, body, and soul. Through these practices, you will discover the profound effects of being fully present, caring for yourself with tenderness, and embracing a compassionate approach towards yourself and others.

Mindfulness invites you to embark on a journey of presence—an invitation to immerse yourself fully in the richness of each moment. It encourages you to let go of the past and future, and instead, anchor yourself in the beauty of the present. Through mindfulness, you cultivate a heightened awareness that allows you to engage with life more deeply, savouring the simple joys, and finding peace amidst the chaos.

Self-care becomes your sacred ritual—a time to honour your well-being and tend to your needs with love and compassion. It is not a luxury but a necessity, a recognition that by caring for yourself, you replenish your inner reserves and create the foundation for a flourishing life. Self-care invites you to embrace practices that nourish your body, mind, and spirit, allowing you to show up fully for yourself and others.

Within the realm of self-compassion, you discover the transformative power of kindness and acceptance towards yourself. It is a gentle reminder that you are human, deserving of love, understanding, and forgiveness. Self-compassion becomes the balm that soothes your inner wounds and nurtures your growth, enabling you to embrace your vulnerabilities with courage and grace.

So, dear seeker of peace, get ready to embark on this transformative chapter where mindfulness, self-care, and self-compassion weave together to form a tapestry of well-being and tranquillity. Embrace the power of the present moment, prioritise your self-care rituals, and let self-compassion guide your way. With each breath, each self-nurturing act, and each gesture of kindness towards yourself, you cultivate a sanctuary of peace that emanates from within and touches every aspect of your life.

Throughout this journey, remember that mindfulness, self-care, and self-compassion are not mere concepts to be understood but practices to be embraced and lived. Allow their wisdom to infuse your daily experiences, guiding you towards a life of authenticity, fulfilment, and serenity. Embrace the transformative power of mindfulness, self-care, and self-compassion, and unlock the boundless potential that awaits within the sanctuary of your being.

Certainly! Here are three inspirational and not-so-obvious techniques for mindfulness, self-care, and self-compassion to nurture your well-being and maintain a sense of peace:

1. Nature Immersion Ritual: Nature holds a profound ability to nurture and restore our well-being. Create a nature immersion ritual by setting aside dedicated time to connect with the natural world. Find a serene outdoor setting, whether it's a nearby park, a peaceful garden, or a tranquil beach. Leave behind distractions and immerse yourself fully in nature's embrace. Engage your senses by noticing the gentle breeze, the sound of birdsong, the texture of the earth beneath your feet. Allow yourself to be present and observe the intricate beauty of nature. As you breathe in the fresh air and take in the sights and sounds, feel a sense of tranquillity wash over you, restoring your inner peace and harmony.

2. Gratitude Happiness Hunt: Infuse your mindfulness practice with a playful twist by embarking on a gratitude happiness hunt. Create a list of gratitude prompts that encourage you to notice and appreciate the small joys and blessings in your surroundings. For example, "Find something blue that brings you joy," or "Discover something in nature that inspires awe." Armed with your list, embark on a journey of mindful exploration, seeking out these prompts in your daily life. As you encounter each item, take a moment to pause, observe, and feel gratitude for the beauty and abundance that surrounds you. This interactive practice not only cultivates mindfulness but also amplifies your sense of gratitude and well-being.

3. Loving-Kindness Adventure: Expand your self-compassion practice by embarking on a loving-kindness adventure. Choose a day or a week dedicated to showering yourself and others with loving-kindness. Each morning, set an intention to approach yourself and those you encounter throughout the day with genuine warmth, kindness, and compassion. Engage in small acts of kindness, such as leaving a heartfelt note for a loved one or offering a helping hand to a stranger. As you practice loving-kindness towards yourself and others, notice how it uplifts your own well-being and creates a ripple effect of positivity and connection. Embrace the adventure of cultivating self-compassion and spreading kindness, knowing that every act of love and compassion contributes to a more peaceful and harmonious world.

By integrating these inspirational techniques into your mindfulness, self-care, and self-compassion practices, you create a holistic approach to nurturing your well-being and maintaining a sense of peace. Embrace the beauty of nature, infuse gratitude into your daily life, and explore the transformative power of loving-kindness. May these practices be your guiding lights on the path to inner peace, reminding you of the boundless wellspring of joy, love, and compassion that resides within you.

In a bustling city filled with hurried footsteps and demanding schedules, there lived a woman named Emily. She was a devoted mother, a dedicated employee, and a pillar of strength for her loved ones. However, in the midst of her responsibilities, Emily often neglected her own well-being, forgetting the importance of self-care and self-compassion.

One day, as Emily's energy waned and stress accumulated, she realised the need for a change. She made a commitment to prioritise self-care and infuse it with a compassionate touch. She decided to embark on a journey of self-discovery and nurturing, recognising that by taking care of herself, she would be able to show up more fully for others.

Emily began by establishing a daily self-care routine that catered to her physical, emotional, and spiritual needs. She set aside time for meditation, journaling, and engaging in activities that brought her joy, such as dancing and painting. Each day, she dedicated a few moments to offer herself words of kindness and love, reminding herself that she was worthy of care and compassion.

As Emily immersed herself in self-care practices, something remarkable happened. She noticed that her newfound sense of self-compassion extended far beyond her own well-being. It began to radiate outwards, touching the lives of those around her.

Her children, who had observed her transformation, started to witness the power of self-care and self-compassion first-hand. They saw their mother embrace her own needs without guilt, setting an example of self-acceptance and self-love. Inspired by her actions, they, too, began prioritising their well-being and cultivating self-compassion.

At work, Emily's newfound sense of balance and self-compassion had a ripple effect. Her colleagues, initially puzzled by her radiant energy, soon discovered that her approach to self-care was contagious. Inspired by her example, they began to carve out time for themselves and started infusing self-compassion into their daily routines. The office environment became a space of support, understanding, and collective well-being.

As Emily continued to nurture herself with compassion, an unexpected outcome unfolded. She discovered that her relationships deepened, as her capacity for empathy and understanding expanded. By meeting her own needs and tending to her inner world with kindness, she found herself better equipped to connect with others on a deeper level. The conversations she had with loved ones became more meaningful, the support she offered became more genuine, and her presence became a source of solace and inspiration.

Through her journey of self-care with compassion, Emily not only transformed her own life but also touched the lives of those around her. She realised that self-care was not a selfish act but a profound act of love and service. By prioritising her own well-being and cultivating self-compassion, she became a beacon of light, illuminating the path for others to do the same.

Emily's story serves as a gentle reminder that self-care and self-compassion have a remarkable way of rippling outwards, creating a positive impact far beyond ourselves. As we nurture ourselves with love and compassion, we not only cultivate inner peace but also contribute to the well-being and happiness of those we encounter along our journey. May Emily's tale inspire us all to embrace self-care with compassion, knowing that our own well-being and the well-being of others are intricately interconnected.

Nurturing your well-being while nourishing your soul and maintaining a sense of peace is a profound endeavour that requires a delicate balance and deep self-awareness. It is an invitation to embark on a transformative journey, where self-care becomes a sacred act and inner peace becomes a guiding compass.

At its core, nurturing your well-being means tending to your physical, emotional, and spiritual needs with love and intention. It means honouring your body as a temple, nourishing it with wholesome foods, movement, and rest. It means acknowledging and expressing your emotions, allowing them to flow freely without judgment or resistance. It means cultivating a connection to your innermost self and nurturing your spirit through practices that resonate with your soul.

Nourishing your soul goes beyond the material realm and dives into the depths of what truly brings you joy and fulfilment. It is a journey of exploration, where you listen attentively to the whispers of your heart and follow the path that ignites your spirit. It may involve engaging in creative pursuits, spending time in nature, or immersing yourself in spiritual practices that resonate with your essence. It is about aligning your actions with your values and living in accordance with your authentic self.

Maintaining a sense of peace requires conscious effort and unwavering commitment. It begins with the cultivation of mindfulness, the art of being fully present in each moment. It involves finding moments of stillness amidst the chaos, allowing yourself to connect with the inner sanctuary of calm that resides within you. It means releasing attachments to outcomes, surrendering to the flow of life, and embracing the impermanence of all things. It means choosing thoughts, words, and actions that align with peace and harmony, both within yourself and in your interactions with others.

As you embark on this profound journey of nurturing your well-being, nourishing your soul, and maintaining a sense of peace, you will uncover the interconnectedness of these elements. You will witness the ways in which tending to your physical, emotional, and spiritual needs enhances your overall well-being. You will discover that by nourishing your soul, you deepen your sense of purpose and fulfilment. And you will realise that inner peace becomes the steady anchor that allows you to navigate the ebb and flow of life with grace and resilience.

There are many ways for a person to nurture their well-being while nourishing their soul and maintaining a sense of peace. One way is to cultivate a holistic and intentional approach to self-care. Here are some key practices to consider:

1. Self-Reflection and Self-Awareness: Take time for self-reflection and cultivate self-awareness. Pause and check in with yourself regularly to identify your needs, emotions, and desires. Listen attentively to your inner voice and honour what it communicates to you. This self-awareness will guide you in making choices that align with your well-being and soul nourishment.

2. Mindfulness and Presence: Embrace the practice of mindfulness, which involves being fully present in each moment without judgment. Cultivate awareness of your thoughts, feelings, and sensations as they arise. Engage in activities with full attention and savour the simple pleasures of life. By anchoring yourself in the present moment, you create space for peace and a deeper connection with your soul.

3. Self-Care Rituals: Prioritise self-care rituals that cater to your physical, emotional, and spiritual needs. Create a self-care routine that includes activities such as exercise, nourishing meals, restful sleep, journaling, meditation, or engaging in hobbies that bring you joy. Tailor your self-care practices to align with what rejuvenates and uplifts your spirit.

4. Soulful Connections: Cultivate meaningful connections with others who uplift and inspire you. Surround yourself with individuals who share similar values and support your growth. Engage in soulful conversations, practice active

listening, and foster authentic relationships that nurture your soul. Seek out community and social support that aligns with your beliefs and desires.

5. Soul Nourishment: Engage in activities that nourish your soul and ignite your passions. Explore creative outlets, such as art, music, writing, or dancing, that allow you to express yourself authentically. Spend time in nature, connecting with the beauty and tranquillity it offers. Engage in spiritual practices or rituals that resonate with your beliefs and cultivate a deeper connection with the essence of your being.

6. Compassionate Self-Reflection: Practice self-compassion and self-forgiveness. Embrace your imperfections and treat yourself with kindness and understanding. When faced with challenges or setbacks, approach yourself with a gentle and compassionate mindset. Treat yourself as you would a dear friend, offering support, encouragement, and love.

Remember, nurturing your well-being while nourishing your soul and maintaining a sense of peace is a continuous journey. Be open to exploring what works best for you and adapt your practices as needed. Trust in your own wisdom and intuition and honour the unique path that unfolds before you. By prioritising self-care, soul nourishment, and peace cultivation, you create a harmonious and fulfilling existence that radiates from within and positively impacts the world around you.

Remember that this journey is unique to you. Embrace the wisdom of self-discovery and self-compassion as you navigate the path. Be gentle with yourself, honouring the ups and downs, the joys, and challenges. Embrace the transformative power of self-care, soul nourishment, and peace cultivation. Embrace the profound realisation that as you nurture your well-being and nourish your soul, you not only create a more fulfilling life for yourself but also become a beacon of light and inspiration for others.

PART 5
TIME AND TRANQUILLITY

Welcome to Part 5: Time and Tranquillity. In this section, we delve into the profound relationship between time and inner peace. We explore the art of slowing down, savouring the present moment, and finding tranquillity amidst the busyness of life. In a world that often prioritises productivity and haste, we invite you to embrace a different perspective—one that values the richness of each passing moment and the serenity that comes with living in harmony with the flow of time. Through mindful practices and a shift in mindset, you will discover the transformative power of embracing time as a precious gift and cultivating tranquillity as a sanctuary within. Get ready to embark on a journey that will help you reclaim your time, nourish your spirit, and awaken a deep sense of peace within your being.

We will cover:

- Time Management Strategies: Exploring effective time management techniques that allow you to work less, optimise productivity, and create more time for the things that matter most to you.
- Prioritising Self-Care and Leisure: Recognising the importance of rest, leisure, and self-care in maintaining a healthy work-life balance and sustaining long-term success.
- Creating Boundaries: Establishing boundaries to protect your time, energy, and overall well-being, enabling you to focus on what truly matters.

CHAPTER 15
TIME AND TRANQUILLITY

In this section, we invite you to explore three fresh and empowering approaches to time management. In a world where time often feels scarce and demands relentlessly pull us in multiple directions, it is crucial to find innovative ways to optimise our time while maintaining a sense of inner tranquillity.

Throughout this section, we will dive deeper into these fresh approaches to time management, offering insights, practical strategies, and mindful practices to help you reclaim your time and cultivate a greater sense of tranquillity. By integrating these innovative approaches into your life, you will create a harmonious relationship with time—one that allows you to make the most of each moment while nurturing your well-being. Get ready to embark on a transformative journey towards time mastery and inner tranquillity.

1. Intentional Time Blocking: Instead of succumbing to the endless to-do list and a constant feeling of being overwhelmed, embrace intentional time blocking. Set aside dedicated blocks of time for specific tasks or activities, allowing you to fully immerse yourself in them without distractions. By prioritising and structuring your time, you create a sense of focus and efficiency while ensuring moments of rest and rejuvenation.

Intentional Time Blocking is a powerful technique that involves setting aside dedicated blocks of time for specific tasks or activities to enhance focus and productivity. Here's how you can practice Intentional Time Blocking:

1. Identify Your Priorities: Start by identifying your key priorities and the tasks that require your attention. This can include work-related projects, personal goals, self-care activities, or any other commitments that hold significance in your life.

2. Allocate Time Blocks: Divide your day into distinct time blocks and assign specific tasks or activities to each block. Consider your energy levels, concentration span, and the nature of the tasks when scheduling. For example, you may designate a morning block for important work projects, an afternoon block for meetings or creative work, and an evening block for personal activities or relaxation.

3. Set Clear Boundaries: During each time block, establish clear boundaries to minimise distractions and interruptions. Communicate your availability to colleagues, family members, or anyone else who may seek your attention during that time. Turn off notifications on your devices, close unnecessary tabs, or apps, and create a conducive environment that supports focus and concentration.

4. Maintain Discipline and Focus: Once you enter a time block, commit to working solely on the assigned task or activity. Stay focused and resist the urge to multitask or switch between different tasks. Use techniques like Pomodoro or timeboxing to break the block into smaller intervals with designated breaks, enhancing productivity and preventing burnout.

5. Adapt and Refine: Regularly review and adjust your time blocks as needed. Reflect on your productivity and the effectiveness of your scheduling. Experiment with different block durations or rearrange tasks to find what works best for you. Be flexible and open to refining your approach based on your evolving needs and circumstances.

Remember, Intentional Time Blocking is a flexible technique that allows you to tailor your schedule to your unique requirements. It helps create structure, maintain focus, and ensure that you allocate dedicated time to the activities that matter most. By implementing this practice, you empower yourself to make intentional choices about how you spend your time and optimise your productivity while maintaining a sense of balance and well-being.

2. Mindful Prioritisation: Shift from a mindset of busyness to one of mindful prioritisation. Take a step back and assess what truly matters to you and aligns with your values. Engage in conscious decision-making by asking yourself: What activities or tasks contribute most meaningfully to my goals and overall well-being? By letting go of nonessential commitments and focusing on what truly matters, you create space for quality experiences and a more balanced and fulfilling life.

Here's a step-by-step process for practicing mindful prioritisation:

1. Self-Reflection: Begin by setting aside some quiet and uninterrupted time for self-reflection. Find a comfortable space where you can focus and connect with your inner self.

2. Clarify Your Values: Reflect on your core values and what truly matters to you in life. Consider what brings you joy, fulfilment, and a sense of purpose. Identifying your values will serve as a guiding framework for your priorities.

3. Assess Current Commitments: Take stock of your current commitments, responsibilities, and activities. Review your schedule, to-do lists, and any ongoing projects. Assess whether each commitment aligns with your values and contributes meaningfully to your goals.

4. Eliminate Nonessential Tasks: Identify tasks or commitments that are not essential or do not align with your values and goals. Be willing to let go of activities that drain your energy or distract you from what truly matters. Give yourself permission to release nonessential tasks from your schedule.

5. Identify High-Impact Activities: Determine which tasks or activities have the most significant impact on your goals and well-being. Consider the outcomes that align with your values and contribute to your long-term vision. Prioritise activities that are meaningful, fulfilling, and in line with your values.

6. Focus on the Essential Few: Embrace the principle of "less is more" by narrowing down your priorities to a manageable number. Avoid overloading your schedule and spreading yourself too thin. Focus on a select few

priorities that truly resonate with your values and have the potential to make a substantial difference.

7. Create a Prioritisation System: Develop a system for organising and prioritising your tasks. This can be as simple as using a digital or physical planner, a task management app, or a journal to track and rank your priorities. Find a method that works best for you and helps you stay organised and focused.

8. Regularly Review and Adjust: Periodically review your priorities and reassess their alignment with your values and goals. Be open to adjusting and realigning as needed, especially as circumstances change or new opportunities arise. Regularly revisit and refine your priorities to ensure they reflect your evolving needs and aspirations.

9. Practice Self-Compassion: Remember to be kind and compassionate toward yourself throughout this process. Avoid judgment or self-criticism if you need to adjust or reprioritise. Practice self-compassion and embrace the understanding that your priorities may shift over time.

By following these steps, you can practice mindful prioritisation and make intentional choices about how you allocate your time and energy. This process empowers you to focus on what truly matters, align your actions with your values, and create a sense of fulfilment and purpose in your daily life.

3. Flow-based Scheduling: Embrace the concept of flow-based scheduling, which revolves around aligning your tasks and activities with your natural energy and focus levels. Observe your own patterns and identify your peak times of productivity, creativity, and mental clarity. Schedule your most important and challenging tasks during these periods, and reserve lighter activities for times when your energy naturally dips. By working in harmony with your own flow, you maximise productivity while maintaining a sense of ease and balance.

Here's a step-by-step process for implementing Flow-Based Scheduling:

1. Observe Your Natural Energy Patterns: Start by observing your natural energy patterns throughout the day. Notice when you feel most alert, focused, and energised, as well as when you tend to experience dips in energy or decreased concentration. Become aware of your own unique rhythm.

2. Identify Your Peak Productivity Times: Based on your observations, identify your peak productivity times—the periods when you feel most energised and mentally sharp. These are the optimal moments to tackle tasks that require high levels of concentration, creativity, or problem-solving skills.

3. Schedule High-Priority Tasks During Peak Times: Once you've identified your peak productivity times, schedule your most important and challenging tasks during these periods. Reserve these blocks of time for focused work on tasks that require your utmost attention and effort. By aligning your high-priority tasks with your peak

productivity, you optimise your performance and enhance your chances of achieving flow.

4. Reserve Lighter Activities for Lower Energy Periods: Recognise the periods when your energy naturally dips or when you may feel less mentally alert. During these times, reserve lighter activities or tasks that don't require as much focus or creativity. This could include responding to emails, organising files, or engaging in routine administrative work.

5. Take Regular Breaks: Integrate regular breaks into your schedule, regardless of your energy levels. Breaks allow for rejuvenation and prevent mental fatigue. Use these moments to stretch, take a short walk, practice deep breathing, or engage in a quick mindfulness exercise. Breaks can help you recharge and sustain your energy levels throughout the day.

6. Stay Present and Engaged: When engaging in tasks, stay present and fully engaged. Minimise distractions, such as notifications or interruptions, and create a focused work environment. Practice mindfulness by bringing your attention to the task at hand and immersing yourself fully in the present moment. This level of attentiveness can help facilitate a state of flow.

7. Evaluate and Adjust: Regularly evaluate the effectiveness of your flow-based schedule. Reflect on your productivity and how well you align tasks with your energy levels. Adjust your schedule as needed, considering any

changes in your energy patterns or work requirements. Be flexible and open to refining your approach based on what works best for you.

A short story to give an insight into flow-based scheduling:

Once upon a time, there was a person named Alex who led a busy and demanding life. Juggling work, family responsibilities, and personal commitments, Alex often felt overwhelmed and time poor. The days seemed to pass by in a blur, leaving little opportunity for focused work or moments of relaxation.

Feeling the need for a change, Alex decided to explore the concept of flow-based scheduling. Intrigued by the idea of aligning tasks with natural energy rhythms, Alex was determined to create a more balanced and productive approach to time management.

Alex began by observing personal energy patterns. After a few days of reflection, it became clear that mornings were when creativity and focus peaked, while late afternoons were often marked by a decrease in energy and mental clarity. Armed with this newfound awareness, Alex crafted a flow-based schedule that embraced these natural rhythms.

Each morning, Alex dedicated the first two hours to high-priority tasks that required intense concentration and creative thinking. During this time, distractions were minimised, and the focus was solely on the task at hand. By capitalising on the peak productivity period, Alex accomplished more in those two hours than ever before.

As the day progressed and energy levels naturally dipped, Alex shifted focus to lighter activities. These included responding to emails, attending meetings, and engaging in administrative tasks that required less mental effort. By intentionally reserving these tasks for lower energy periods, Alex ensured that precious mental resources were conserved and used efficiently.

To maintain a healthy work-life balance, Alex incorporated regular breaks into the schedule. These breaks allowed for rejuvenation, physical movement, and moments of mindfulness. Whether it was a short walk outside, a few minutes of deep breathing, or a quick meditation session, these breaks served as opportunities to recharge and reset, preventing burnout, and fostering a sense of well-being.

Over time, Alex noticed a remarkable transformation. The flow-based schedule not only enhanced productivity but also brought a newfound sense of harmony and fulfilment. By working in sync with personal energy rhythms, Alex experienced a state of flow—a seamless and focused immersion in tasks that felt effortless and rewarding. The once time-poor individual now had a greater sense of control over time, with moments of both productivity and tranquillity woven into the day.

But the most surprising outcome of flow-based scheduling was the ripple effect it had on other aspects of Alex's life. By embracing the power of intentional time management, Alex found that there was more room for meaningful connections, self-care, and pursuing personal passions. Relationships flourished, and a renewed sense of purpose emerged, as time was intentionally carved out for the things that truly mattered.

With flow-based scheduling as their guiding principle, Alex's life underwent a remarkable transformation. Time became a source of empowerment, not a source of stress. By embracing the natural ebb and flow of energy, Alex not only achieved greater productivity but also nurtured well-being, leading a life that felt more balanced, purposeful, and fulfilling.

And so, Alex's journey with flow-based scheduling serves as a testament to the transformative power of aligning tasks with personal energy rhythms. It reminds us all that when we work in harmony with our natural flow, time becomes a friend rather than a foe, and our days become an exquisite dance of productivity and tranquillity.

Remember, flow-based scheduling is a flexible approach that allows you to optimise your productivity and well-being by working in harmony with your natural energy rhythms. By scheduling tasks during your peak productivity times and reserving lighter activities for lower energy periods, you create a work schedule that maximises focus, engagement, and satisfaction. Embrace the fluidity of this approach and adjust it as necessary to meet your evolving needs.

CHAPTER 16
PRIORITISING SELF-CARE AND LEISURE

In this section, we delve into the profound significance of rest, leisure, and self-care in maintaining a healthy work-life balance and sustaining long-term success. In a world that often glorifies busyness and constant productivity, it's crucial to recognise the value of prioritising our well-being and allowing ourselves moments of rejuvenation and leisure.

Remember, by prioritising self-care and leisure, you are not only investing in yourself but also creating a solid foundation for a fulfilling and harmonious life. So, join us on this journey as we explore the transformative power of self-care and leisure, empowering you to prioritise your well-being and cultivate a life of sustainable success and happiness.

In this section we will gain some insightful perspectives, practical strategies, and transformative practices to help you prioritise self-care and leisure. We will debunk the myth that constant productivity is the only path to success and guide you toward a more balanced and fulfilling approach. Get ready to embrace the wisdom of self-care, indulge in leisure, and discover the profound impact they can have on your overall well-being and sustained success.

1. Rest as a Productivity Enhancer: Contrary to popular belief, rest is not a hindrance to success but a catalyst for it. Research has shown that adequate rest, including quality sleep and regular breaks, improves cognitive function, enhances creativity, and boosts overall productivity. By prioritising rest, we can achieve optimal

performance and prevent burnout, ensuring sustainable success in the long run.

2. Leisure as a Source of Inspiration: Engaging in leisure activities that bring us joy and fulfilment is not a frivolous indulgence but a vital source of inspiration and personal growth. Taking time to pursue hobbies, explore new interests, or simply unwind allows us to tap into our creativity, gain fresh perspectives, and replenish our energy. Leisure provides the space for self-discovery and rejuvenation, fuelling our well-being and enhancing our ability to excel in other areas of life.

3. Self-Care as a Necessity, Not an Option: Prioritising self-care is not selfish; it is a fundamental act of self-respect and compassion. Engaging in self-care practices, such as mindfulness, exercise, healthy eating, and nurturing relationships, nourishes our physical, emotional, and mental well-being. It equips us with the resilience and energy needed to navigate life's challenges and maintain a positive outlook.

Here are some facts on the importance of rest, leisure, and self-care:

1. Rest and Sleep:

- Quality sleep is crucial for cognitive function, memory consolidation, and overall well-being. It enhances creativity, problem-solving abilities, and emotional regulation.

- Lack of sleep or poor sleep quality can impair judgment, decrease productivity, and contribute to physical and mental health issues such as increased stress, decreased immune function, and higher risk of chronic conditions like heart disease and diabetes.

- Taking regular breaks throughout the day, even short ones, can improve focus, attention, and productivity. It allows the brain to rest and recharge, leading to better overall performance.

2. Leisure and Recreation:

- Engaging in leisure activities reduces stress levels and promotes mental well-being. It provides an opportunity for relaxation, enjoyment, and personal fulfilment.
- Participating in leisure activities can improve physical health by increasing physical activity, reducing the risk of chronic diseases, and enhancing cardiovascular fitness.
- Leisure activities foster creativity, problem-solving skills, and cognitive flexibility. They

offer an outlet for self-expression and can lead to personal growth and self-discovery.

3. Self-Care:

- Self-care practices, such as mindfulness, exercise, and healthy eating, are essential for maintaining physical, mental, and emotional well-being.
- Prioritising self-care reduces the risk of burnout and increases resilience to stress. It promotes a positive mindset, self-compassion, and improved overall quality of life.
- Nurturing relationships and social connections is a crucial aspect of self-care. Meaningful connections contribute to feelings of belonging, support, and happiness.

4. Work-Life Balance:

- Achieving a healthy work-life balance is vital for overall well-being and prevents the negative effects of chronic stress and burnout.
- Balancing work with leisure, hobbies, and personal time improves job satisfaction, productivity, and creativity.
- Taking breaks and setting boundaries between work and personal life enhances mental clarity, reduces fatigue, and boosts overall happiness and satisfaction.

Here are two exercises to help you achieve mental recharge and energisation:

1. Mindful Breathing Exercise:

    1. Find a quiet and comfortable space where you can sit or lie down.
    2. Close your eyes and take a few deep breaths, allowing your body to relax and release any tension.
    3. Bring your attention to your breath and begin to observe each inhale and exhale.
    4. Take slow, deep breaths, counting to four as you inhale and counting to four as you exhale.
    5. As you continue to breathe, focus your attention on the sensation of the breath entering and leaving your body.
    6. If your mind wanders, gently bring your focus back to the breath without judgment.
    7. Engage in this mindful breathing exercise for at least 5-10 minutes, allowing yourself to fully immerse in the present moment and recharge your mental energy.

2. Movement Break:

1. Stand up and move away from your workspace or current environment.
2. Engage in a brief physical activity that gets your blood flowing and invigorates your body. This could be a quick walk, a set of stretching exercises, or even a dance break.
3. As you move, bring your attention to the physical sensations in your body—feel the muscles stretching, the blood circulating, and the energy flowing.
4. Embrace the opportunity to disconnect from your thoughts and focus solely on the movement and sensations in your body.
5. Allow yourself to fully enjoy the physical activity and let go of any mental tension or stress.
6. Engaging in a movement break for even just a few minutes can provide a mental recharge, increase energy levels, and enhance overall well-being.

Remember, these exercises are designed to help you recharge mentally and boost your energy levels. Incorporate them into your daily routine as needed to take intentional breaks, refocus your mind, and revitalise your energy. Adjust the exercises to suit your preferences and physical capabilities, and most importantly, enjoy the process of recharging your mental energy and finding a renewed sense of vitality.

It is worth reminding oneself that rest, leisure, and self-care are not indulgences but necessary components of a healthy and fulfilling life. By prioritising these aspects, you can enhance your well-being, improve productivity, and sustain long-term success. Take time for rest, engage in enjoyable activities, and practice self-care to nurture your mind, body, and soul.

CHAPTER 17
CREATING BOUNDARIES

Welcome to Creating Boundaries. In this section, we explore the power of establishing boundaries to protect your time, energy, and overall well-being. By setting clear and healthy boundaries, you can create a nurturing environment that allows you to focus on what truly matters and maintain a sense of balance in your life.

Remember, creating boundaries is an act of self-care and self-respect. It empowers you to protect your time, energy, and overall well-being, enabling you to focus on what truly matters. By defining priorities, learning to say no, designating sacred time, establishing digital boundaries, and communicating your boundaries effectively, you create a balanced and fulfilling life that honours your needs and values.

So, join us on this journey of boundary setting as we explore practical strategies, empowering insights, and transformative practices that will empower you to create boundaries that support your well-being and allow you to live a life of clarity, purpose, and fulfilment. Here are some boundary setting 'Musts'.

1. Define Your Priorities: Start by gaining clarity on your priorities. Reflect on what truly matters to you—your values, goals, and the activities that bring you joy and fulfilment. With a clear understanding of your priorities, you can establish boundaries that align with your values and support your overall well-being.

2. Learn to Say No: One of the most powerful ways to create boundaries is by learning to say no. Saying no to commitments, tasks, or requests that do not align with your priorities or drain your energy allows you to free up time and resources for the things that truly matter. Practice asserting your boundaries with kindness and assertiveness, knowing that it is a necessary act of self-care.

3. Designate Sacred Time: Carve out sacred time in your schedule dedicated to activities that rejuvenate and nourish you. This could be a regular exercise routine, time for self-reflection, engaging in a hobby, or simply disconnecting from technology. Protect this time fiercely and honour its importance in replenishing your energy and maintaining your overall well-being.

4. Establish Digital Boundaries: In today's digital age, it is essential to establish boundaries around technology and screen time. Set limits on your use of social media, email, and other digital distractions. Create designated technology-free zones or specific times of the day when you disconnect from devices to foster presence, reduce stress, and enhance your ability to focus on meaningful activities.

5. Communicate Your Boundaries: Clearly communicate your boundaries with others, whether it's with family, friends, or colleagues. Express your needs and expectations respectfully and assertively. Effective communication allows others to understand and respect your boundaries, fostering healthier and more supportive relationships.

Here are two fresh exercises to help you establish boundaries:

1. Boundary Visualisation:

- Find a quiet and comfortable space where you can sit and relax.

- Close your eyes and take a few deep breaths to centre yourself.

- Visualise yourself surrounded by a protective bubble or shield.

- Imagine this bubble as a representation of your personal space and boundaries.

- As you envision the bubble, imagine it becoming stronger, impenetrable, and clearly defined.

- See yourself within this bubble, feeling safe, empowered, and in control of your personal boundaries.

- Take a moment to set the intention that this bubble represents your commitment to honouring your boundaries and protecting your well-being.

- Whenever you need to reinforce your boundaries or assert yourself, visualise this bubble and draw strength from it.

2. Boundary Declaration Letter:

- Set aside some time to write a boundary declaration letter to yourself.

- Start by acknowledging the importance of boundaries in your life and well-being.

- Reflect on specific areas or situations where you feel your boundaries are being challenged or violated.

- Write a letter to yourself, clearly stating your boundaries, needs, and expectations in those situations.

- Be assertive and specific about what you will and will not tolerate.

- Express your commitment to honouring and enforcing these boundaries, as well as the positive impact they will have on your well-being.

- Seal the letter in an envelope and keep it in a safe place.

- Whenever you need a reminder of your boundaries, reread the letter to reaffirm your commitment to yourself and your well-being.

These exercises aim to help you establish and reinforce your boundaries in creative and engaging ways. Remember, boundaries are an essential part of self-care and maintaining a healthy work-life balance. Embrace these exercises as tools to empower yourself, protect your well-being, and create a harmonious and fulfilling life that respects your needs and values.

Once upon a time, there was a woman named Maya who had always been a people pleaser. She had a hard time saying no and often found herself overwhelmed by the demands and expectations of others. Maya was always putting everyone else's needs before her own, sacrificing her time, energy, and well-being in the process.

One day, Maya realised that she needed to make a change. She had reached a breaking point where she felt drained, stressed, and unfulfilled. She knew deep down that she deserved better, and it was time to establish healthy boundaries to protect her time, energy, and overall well-being.

Maya began by reflecting on her priorities and values. She recognised that she needed to prioritise her own needs and happiness in order to live a fulfilling life. With this newfound clarity, she took a deep breath and made a commitment to herself.

The first step Maya took was learning to say no. She started setting boundaries with her friends, family, and colleagues. She politely declined invitations and requests that didn't align with her priorities or drained her energy. Maya discovered that saying no wasn't selfish; it was an act of self-care and self-respect.

As Maya continued to establish boundaries, she noticed a remarkable shift in her life. She had more time and energy to invest in activities that brought her joy and fulfilment. She began pursuing hobbies, nurturing her relationships with loved ones, and focusing on her own personal growth. Maya felt a newfound sense of freedom and empowerment.

Not only did Maya's boundaries positively impact her personal life, but they also had a remarkable effect on her professional life. She became more assertive in the workplace, setting clear expectations and boundaries with her colleagues and superiors. Maya found that by creating boundaries, she was able to work more efficiently, maintain a healthy work-life balance, and achieve better results.

As Maya continued her journey of boundary-setting, she noticed a transformation within herself. She felt a renewed sense of confidence, inner peace, and self-respect. Maya realised that establishing boundaries was not only about protecting her time and energy but also about honouring her worth and valuing herself.

Others noticed the positive changes in Maya as well. They respected her boundaries and admired her self-assuredness. Maya's relationships became healthier and more balanced, as she nurtured connections that were based on mutual respect and understanding.

With her newfound boundaries, Maya created a life that was aligned with her values and brought her deep contentment. She no longer felt overwhelmed or depleted. Instead, she embraced a sense of harmony and fulfilment, knowing that she had reclaimed her power and created a life that honoured her needs and well-being.

Maya's journey serves as an inspiration to all who seek to establish healthy boundaries. It is a reminder that by setting boundaries, we can transform our lives, reclaim our time and energy, and cultivate a sense of inner peace and self-empowerment.

PART 6
MONEY MASTERY & MANIFESTING

Welcome to Money Mastery. In this section, we embark on a journey of transforming our relationship with money and developing a mindset of abundance. Through empowering mindset shifts, cultivating abundance consciousness, and adopting smart money habits, we can manifest greater financial abundance and create a solid foundation for wealth and success.

1. Money Mindset Shifts:

We begin by exploring the power of our mindset and its influence on our financial reality. By identifying and transforming limiting beliefs and negative associations surrounding money, we can unlock our true potential for wealth and abundance. It's time to release any scarcity thinking and embrace a mindset that aligns with prosperity, abundance, and limitless possibilities.

2. Embracing Abundance Consciousness:

In this chapter, we delve deeper into cultivating a mindset of abundance. By nurturing positive thoughts, intentions, and actions, we align ourselves with the flow of abundance in all areas of our lives, including our finances. We discover the power of gratitude, visualisation, and affirmations to attract wealth and abundance into our reality. It's time to embrace a new level of consciousness and welcome the limitless abundance that awaits us.

3. Smart Money Habits:

Building and sustaining wealth requires practical strategies and smart money habits. In this chapter, we explore the foundations of financial success, including budgeting, investing, and creating multiple streams of income. We learn how to make informed financial decisions, set realistic financial goals, and cultivate a healthy relationship with money. By adopting smart money habits, we empower ourselves to create a solid financial future and achieve our long-term financial aspirations.

Through these transformative chapters, we unlock the secrets to money mastery and abundance. We invite you to embark on this journey of self-discovery and growth as we shift our money mindset, embrace abundance consciousness, and develop smart money habits. Together, we will create a prosperous and fulfilling financial future. Get ready to manifest greater financial abundance and experience the freedom and possibilities that come with it.

CHAPTER 18
MONEY MINDSET SHIFTS

Welcome to the transformative journey of Money Mindset Shifts. In this chapter, we delve into the power of identifying and transforming limiting beliefs and negative associations surrounding money. By embarking on this inner exploration, you will empower yourself to manifest greater financial abundance and unlock your true wealth potential. Get ready to challenge old patterns, embrace new possibilities, and welcome a prosperous future.

1. Money Belief Inventory:

Take a moment to reflect on your current beliefs and attitudes towards money. Grab a pen and paper and write down any limiting beliefs or negative associations you have about money. These could include statements such as "Money is hard to come by," "I'll never be wealthy," or "Money is the root of all evil." Take your time and be honest with yourself as you identify these beliefs.

Once you have your list, examine each belief, and question its validity. Challenge the negative narratives and explore alternative, empowering beliefs. For each limiting belief, reframe it into a positive and empowering statement. For example, "Money flows easily and abundantly into my life" or "I deserve to be financially successful."

Here's an example of someone who does a money belief inventory and uncovers some unexpected beliefs that were sabotaging them:

Meet Sarah, a hardworking individual with ambitious career goals. She's always been dedicated and driven, but she finds herself struggling to make significant financial progress. Feeling frustrated and stuck, Sarah decides to delve into her money beliefs to uncover any hidden obstacles that may be holding her back.

As Sarah sits down with pen and paper, she starts writing down her current beliefs and associations with money. She finds the process insightful and begins to realise that her beliefs go beyond the surface level.

One unexpected belief that Sarah uncovers is the idea that "money is a limited resource." Growing up, she witnessed her parents constantly worrying about finances and living pay cheque to pay cheque. This upbringing instilled a scarcity mindset within her, leading her to believe that there will never be enough money to go around. This belief unknowingly held her back from fully embracing financial opportunities and abundance.

Another surprising belief that Sarah discovers is the belief that "money is inherently evil." This belief stems from societal conditioning and cultural influences that have portrayed wealth as a negative force. Sarah realises that she had internalised this belief and, as a result, felt guilt and shame around desiring financial success. This underlying belief sabotaged her progress and prevented her from fully embracing her potential.

Upon recognising these limiting beliefs, Sarah decides to challenge and transform them. She replaces the belief that "money is a limited resource" with the empowering belief that "money flows abundantly and freely into my life." She reframes the belief that "money is inherently evil" into the empowering belief that "money is a tool for positive impact and personal growth."

By consciously working on shifting her money beliefs, Sarah opens herself up to new possibilities and opportunities. She notices a shift in her financial reality as she embraces a mindset of abundance and removes the self-imposed limitations that held her back. With these newfound empowering beliefs, Sarah feels more aligned with her financial goals and experiences a renewed sense of confidence and motivation.

This example illustrates how a money belief inventory can uncover unexpected beliefs that sabotage our financial progress. By shining a light on these limiting beliefs and consciously transforming them, we can overcome internal obstacles and create a more empowering money mindset that supports our financial growth and success.

By taking inventory of your money beliefs and consciously reshaping them, you are taking the first step towards transforming your mindset and inviting greater financial abundance into your life.

2. Abundance Affirmations:

Affirmations are powerful tools for shifting your mindset and attracting what you desire. Create a list of abundance affirmations that resonate with you. These are positive statements that reinforce your belief in your ability to manifest financial abundance. For example, "I am a magnet for money," "I am worthy of unlimited prosperity," or "I attract wealth and abundance effortlessly."

Repeat these affirmations daily, preferably in the morning or before going to bed. Say them with conviction and truly embody the feelings of abundance as you do so. Visualise yourself living in a state of financial abundance, experiencing the joy and freedom it brings. By consistently affirming your abundance mindset, you are programming your subconscious mind to align with wealth and attract greater financial opportunities.

3. Rewrite Your Money Story:

Our beliefs and associations with money often stem from the stories we've heard or experienced throughout our lives. Take some time to reflect on the money stories you've been told or the experiences that have shaped your relationship with money.

Now, consider rewriting your money story. Imagine a new narrative that empowers you and aligns with your desired financial reality. Create a story that highlights your abundance, resourcefulness, and financial success. Be detailed and vivid as you paint a picture of your ideal financial life. Write this new story as if it is already happening, using present tense language.

Read your rewritten money story regularly, allowing it to inspire and guide you towards your financial goals. By rewriting your money story, you are reclaiming the power to shape your financial destiny and creating a positive foundation for attracting greater abundance into your life.

Here's an example of a money story being rewritten:

Meet John, a hardworking individual who has always struggled with financial scarcity and a belief that money is elusive and difficult to come by. Determined to change his financial reality, John decides to rewrite his money story and create a new narrative that aligns with his desired financial abundance.

Previously, John's money story was filled with struggle and lack. He would constantly reinforce beliefs such as "I never have enough money," "Money is hard to earn," and "I'm not destined for wealth." These limiting beliefs held him back from fully embracing opportunities and experiencing financial prosperity.

With a newfound understanding of the power of rewriting his money story, John begins to envision a different narrative. He starts by imagining a life where financial abundance flows effortlessly to him. He sees himself confidently earning, managing, and growing his wealth. He feels the excitement and joy that comes with financial freedom.

As John puts pen to paper, he writes his new money story with conviction and positivity. He includes details about his successful career, wise financial decisions, and the impact he's making through his wealth. He describes the feeling of abundance, generosity, and security that permeates every aspect of his life.

John's rewritten money story reads something like this:

"I am a magnet for financial abundance. Money flows easily and consistently into my life. I am blessed with opportunities to earn and create wealth doing what I love. I make wise financial decisions and confidently invest in my future. With my growing wealth, I create a life of joy, freedom, and purpose. I have more than enough to meet my needs and generously support causes that align with my values. My wealth allows me to make a positive impact in the world and leave a lasting legacy for future generations. I am worthy of unlimited financial success, and I embrace it fully."

John reads his rewritten money story, he feels a surge of inspiration and empowerment. This new narrative replaces the old patterns of scarcity and limitation with a mindset of abundance and possibility. He now believes in his own capacity to create wealth and attract financial opportunities.

With his rewritten money story as a guiding light, John begins to take inspired action aligned with his new beliefs. He starts seeking out new income streams, investing wisely, and adopting healthy money habits. As he consistently lives out his rewritten money story, he witnesses a transformation in his financial reality. Opportunities arise, income increases, and he experiences a greater sense of financial peace and security.

Through rewriting his money story, John has reclaimed his power to shape his financial destiny. He understands that his beliefs and narratives around money play a crucial role in his financial outcomes. With his new empowering money story, John opens himself up to unlimited possibilities and paves the way for a prosperous and abundant financial future.

Through these empowering exercises, you are embarking on a transformative journey of shifting your money mindset. By identifying and transforming limiting beliefs, affirming abundance, and rewriting your money story, you are paving the way for greater financial abundance and prosperity. Get ready to manifest your dreams and create a new narrative of financial success.

CHAPTER 19
ABUNDANCE CONSCIOUSNESS

Welcome to the enlightening journey of Embracing Abundance Consciousness. In this chapter, we dive into the transformative practice of cultivating a mindset of abundance and attracting wealth through positive thoughts, intentions, and actions. By embracing abundance consciousness, you have the power to shift your perception of wealth and manifest the financial abundance you desire. Get ready to embark on a journey of inner transformation and unlock the doors to limitless possibilities.

1. Gratitude Journaling:

One of the most powerful techniques for cultivating abundance consciousness is through the practice of gratitude journaling. Each day, take a few moments to reflect on the blessings and abundance in your life. Write down three to five things that you are grateful for, focusing on both the big and small joys. It could be a loving relationship, good health, a fulfilling job, or even a beautiful sunset.

As you write, immerse yourself in the feeling of gratitude and appreciation. Allow these positive emotions to expand within you. By consistently acknowledging and appreciating the abundance already present in your life, you shift your focus from lack to abundance. This practice trains your mind to recognise and attract more abundance into your experience.

2. Visualisation and Affirmations:

Visualisation and affirmations are powerful tools for creating a mindset of abundance. We have discussed these previously. Take a few moments each day to visualise your desired financial abundance and success. Imagine yourself living a life of wealth, freedom, and fulfilment. Visualise the experiences, possessions, and opportunities that align with your vision of abundance. As you visualise, engage all your senses, and truly feel the emotions of joy, gratitude, and excitement as if your vision is already a reality.

Combine visualisation with affirmations to reinforce your abundance consciousness. Create positive affirmations that reflect your desired financial reality. Repeat them with conviction and belief. For example, "I am a magnet for abundance and prosperity," "I attract wealth and opportunities effortlessly," or "Money flows to me abundantly from multiple sources."

Through consistent practice, visualisation, and affirmations, you are rewiring your subconscious mind to align with abundance. This helps you attract the people, circumstances, and opportunities that support your financial goals.

3. Act as If:

To further embrace abundance consciousness, practice acting as if you already have the abundance you desire. Engage in activities and make choices that align with the mindset of abundance. This could mean treating yourself to something special, making a generous contribution to a cause you believe in, or investing in personal or professional development.

When you act as if you already have abundance, you create a vibrational match with the energy of abundance. This sends a powerful message to the universe and opens channels for greater wealth and opportunities to flow into your life. Remember, it's not about living beyond your means but about embodying the mindset of abundance and making choices that support your financial growth and well-being.

A short 'Act as if…' story

Once upon a time, in a small town nestled in the mountains, there lived a woman named Maya. Maya had always dreamed of financial abundance, but her current circumstances seemed far from her desired reality. She worked tirelessly at a job that paid the bills but didn't fulfil her deepest aspirations.

One day, as Maya sat pondering her dreams, she came across a book that spoke of the power of "acting as if" to attract abundance. Intrigued by the concept, Maya decided to give it a try. She committed to embodying the mindset of abundance and making choices that reflected her desired financial reality.

With newfound determination, Maya began to shift her approach to life. She started by upgrading her appearance. She dressed in clothes that made her feel confident and successful, even if they were not the most expensive ones. Maya noticed that as she carried herself with grace and poise, people responded to her differently. Opportunities seemed to appear out of nowhere, as if the universe was responding to her shift in energy.

Next, Maya decided to invest in her personal growth and education. She enrolled in online courses and attended workshops that aligned with her interests and goals. She immersed herself in learning, expanding her knowledge, and honing her skills. Maya's newfound dedication to personal development opened doors to connections, collaborations, and even job offers she had never expected.

But it wasn't just about personal growth; Maya also wanted to contribute and make a difference in the world. Inspired by her abundance mindset, she started volunteering her time and resources to causes she cared deeply about. She donated to local charities, organised fundraisers, and lent a helping hand wherever she could. Through her acts of generosity, Maya discovered that abundance was not only about wealth but also about the impact she could make in the lives of others.

As Maya continued to "act as if" she already had abundance, something remarkable began to happen. She noticed that her financial situation started to improve. New opportunities for advancement came her way, and her income steadily increased. Maya's relationships flourished as well. She attracted like-minded individuals who supported her vision and celebrated her success.

With each passing day, Maya became more attuned to the energy of abundance that flowed through her life. She recognised that the act of "acting as if" was not about pretending or living beyond her means, but about embodying the mindset and making choices that aligned with her desired financial reality. Maya's actions were a reflection of her faith in the abundance of the universe and her unwavering belief in her own worthiness of financial success.

Through her journey of "acting as if," Maya discovered that abundance wasn't just a destination but a way of being. It was about cultivating a mindset of prosperity, making choices that aligned with her desires, and embracing the opportunities that came her way. As Maya basked in the joy of her newfound abundance, she realised that the transformation had occurred from within. She had unlocked the door to financial prosperity by simply acting as if she already had it. And in doing so, she had opened herself up to a world of endless possibilities and unlimited abundance.

By incorporating these insightful techniques into your daily life, you will cultivate a mindset of abundance and attract greater wealth. Through gratitude journaling, visualisation and affirmations, and acting as if, you are aligning yourself with the abundant flow of the universe. Get ready to experience the transformative power of abundance consciousness and manifest the financial abundance you deserve.

CHAPTER 20
SMART MONEY HABITS

Welcome to the insightful realm of Smart Money Habits. In this chapter, we delve into practical financial strategies that empower you to build and sustain wealth. By implementing these strategies, including budgeting, investing, and creating multiple streams of income, you will gain the knowledge and tools to take control of your financial future and create lasting prosperity. Get ready to embark on a journey of financial empowerment and unlock the path to financial abundance.

1. Budgeting Bliss:

Budgeting is the foundation of sound financial management. Take the time to create a comprehensive budget that aligns with your financial goals and priorities. Start by listing all your sources of income and categorising your expenses. Be diligent in tracking your spending and adjust as needed. Consider allocating a portion of your income towards savings and investments to cultivate a habit of wealth-building. Remember, budgeting is not about restriction but about conscious decision-making and ensuring your money is working for you.

2. Mindful Spending:

Adopt a mindful approach to your spending habits. Before making a purchase, ask yourself if it aligns with your financial goals and priorities. Is it a necessity or a fleeting desire? Practicing delayed gratification and making intentional choices will help you avoid impulsive purchases and redirect your resources towards what truly matters. Embrace the concept of value-based spending, where your money is allocated towards experiences and items that bring long-term fulfilment rather than short-lived pleasure.

3. Investment Mastery:

Explore the world of investing to make your money work for you. Educate yourself on different investment vehicles such as stocks, bonds, mutual funds, real estate, and entrepreneurship. Consider consulting with a financial advisor who can guide you in creating an investment portfolio tailored to your risk tolerance and financial goals. Start small and gradually increase your investments as your knowledge and confidence grow. Remember, investing is a long-term game that requires patience, research, and a diversified approach.

4. Multiple Streams of Income:

Diversify your sources of income to build resilience and create wealth. Explore opportunities for side hustles, freelance work, or entrepreneurship. Leverage your skills, talents, and passions to generate additional income streams. Embrace the digital age and explore online platforms that allow you to monetise your expertise or hobbies. Creating multiple streams of income not only increases your financial stability but also opens doors for personal and professional growth.

5. Financial Education:

Continuously invest in your financial education. Read books, listen to podcasts, and attend seminars or workshops that expand your knowledge of personal finance and wealth management. Stay updated on market trends, economic indicators, and investment strategies. Educate yourself on topics such as tax planning, retirement planning, and debt management. The more you know, the better equipped you'll be to make informed financial decisions and seize opportunities for financial growth.

Here is a fun little story to illustrate budgeting bliss and mindful spending:

Once upon a time in the bustling city of Financia, there lived a man named Alex. Alex had always dreamed of financial stability and freedom, but he often found himself struggling to make ends meet. Determined to turn his financial situation around, he decided to embark on a journey of budgeting bliss and mindful spending.

Alex began by creating a detailed budget that outlined his income and expenses. He meticulously tracked every dollar that came in and went out, ensuring that he had a clear understanding of his financial landscape. Armed with this newfound knowledge, Alex started to make conscious decisions about his spending.

One day, as he wandered through the busy streets of Financia, Alex stumbled upon a tempting electronics store. He was immediately drawn to a sleek and shiny new gadget that he had been eyeing for months. As he held it in his hands, he felt the thrill of instant gratification welling up inside him. However, a voice in the back of his mind reminded him of his commitment to mindful spending.

Taking a deep breath, Alex paused to reflect on his financial goals and priorities. He realised that this impulsive purchase would not align with his long-term aspirations. Instead, he chose to practice delayed gratification and put the gadget back on the shelf. It was a small victory, but it marked the beginning of a transformative shift in his mind-set.

As the days turned into weeks and weeks into months, Alex continued to embrace mindful spending. He became intentional about his purchases, asking himself if they truly added value to his life and aligned with his financial goals. He discovered the joy of finding alternative, more affordable options that still brought him fulfilment.

In his quest for financial stability, Alex also learned to differentiate between his needs and wants. He became adept at distinguishing between necessary expenses and frivolous desires. By prioritising his needs and cutting back on unnecessary expenditures, he found that he had more money to allocate towards his savings and investments.

With each passing month, Alex's financial situation began to improve. He watched as his savings account grew and his debt diminished. The feeling of empowerment and control he experienced was unlike anything he had felt before. He realised that budgeting bliss and mindful spending were not just about restriction but about aligning his financial choices with his dreams and aspirations.

As his financial journey progressed, Alex shared his newfound wisdom with his friends and family. He organised budgeting workshops and shared tips on mindful spending. His enthusiasm and passion for financial empowerment were contagious, and many people in Financia started to adopt his practices.

Over time, Alex transformed from a man burdened by financial stress into a beacon of financial wisdom and stability. His commitment to budgeting bliss and mindful spending not only changed his life but also inspired others to take control of their own financial destinies.

In the end, Alex's story taught us that by embracing budgeting bliss and practicing mindful spending, we have the power to transform our financial realities. With conscious choices and a clear understanding of our financial goals, we can build a solid foundation for a prosperous and fulfilling future.

By adopting these smart money habits, you are setting yourself on a path to financial independence and long-term wealth. Embrace the power of budgeting, practice mindful spending, explore investment opportunities, create multiple streams of income, and invest in your financial education. Together, these strategies will empower you to build and sustain wealth, providing you with the financial freedom and security you desire.

PART 7
INFECTIOUS FINANCIAL ENTHUSIASM

Welcome to the exhilarating realm of Infectious Financial Enthusiasm! In this final section of our journey, we dive into the power of inspiring others, leading by example, and spreading financial literacy. As you embrace your own financial success and abundance, you have the incredible opportunity to ignite a spark in others, empowering them to embark on their own path to wealth and fulfilment.

1. Inspiring Others:

Your financial journey is not just about personal achievement—it's about uplifting and empowering others. By openly sharing your successes, lessons, and experiences, you can inspire those around you to dream bigger, set higher goals, and believe in their own potential for financial abundance. Your enthusiasm becomes contagious, igniting a fire within them to pursue their own financial dreams with unwavering determination.

2. Leading by Example:

As you cultivate infectious financial enthusiasm, you become a shining example of what's possible. Your passion, purpose, and prosperity align to create a beacon of inspiration that others can look up to. By showcasing how your journey has transformed your life, you inspire others to take charge of their own financial destinies. Your commitment to living a life of abundance and fulfilment becomes a catalyst for positive change in their lives.

3. Spreading Financial Literacy:

One of the most powerful ways to empower others is by advocating for financial education. As you deepen your own knowledge and understanding of personal finance, you have the opportunity to share that wisdom with those around you. By equipping others with the tools and knowledge to make informed financial decisions, you help them navigate the complexities of money management and build a solid foundation for long-term success.

By embracing the role of an infectious financial enthusiast, you become a catalyst for positive transformation in the lives of others. Your passion, enthusiasm, and commitment to financial abundance inspire others to believe in themselves, act, and create their own prosperous futures. Together, we can create a world where financial empowerment is the norm, and everyone has the tools and knowledge to thrive.

As we embark on this final leg of our journey, remember that your infectious financial enthusiasm has the power to create a ripple effect of positive change. Embrace your role as an inspiring leader, a beacon of light in the realm of personal finance, and a champion of financial literacy. Let's spread the joy of abundance and inspire others to unlock their own financial potential. Together, we can create a world where financial success is not just a dream but a reality for all.

CHAPTER 21
INSPIRING OTHERS

Sharing your financial journey, successes, and lessons with others, inspiring and empowering them to embrace their own path to wealth and fulfilment.

Get ready to step into the exhilarating realm of inspiring others! In this section, we explore the power of sharing your financial journey, successes, and lessons with others, becoming a catalyst for their own path to wealth and fulfilment. Your experiences and wisdom have the incredible potential to ignite a fire within others, empowering them to believe in their own financial potential. Let's dive into three infectiously inspiring exercises that will energise individuals on their own financial journeys:

1. Personal Success Story Showcase:

Gather a group of friends, family, or like-minded individuals for a personal success story showcase. Each participant takes turns sharing their financial journey, highlighting their successes, challenges, and the valuable lessons they've learned along the way. This exercise not only allows you to celebrate your own accomplishments but also inspires and empowers others by showing them what's possible. As you listen to each person's story, offer genuine support, encouragement, and actionable advice to help them overcome their own obstacles and pursue their dreams.

As an example:

Once upon a time, in a small community filled with individuals aspiring for financial success, there was a woman named Maya. Maya had faced her fair share of financial challenges and setbacks throughout her life, but she never let them dampen her spirit. Determined to turn her circumstances around, Maya embarked on a journey of personal growth, financial education, and unwavering perseverance.

One day, a local community centre organised a Success Story Showcase, where individuals were invited to share their financial journeys and inspire others with their achievements. Maya saw this as an opportunity to not only celebrate her own successes but also uplift and empower those who were still navigating their way to financial prosperity.

As Maya took the stage, she opened up about her early struggles with debt, lack of financial literacy, and the limiting beliefs that held her back. With each word she spoke, she painted a vivid picture of her transformation—a journey that led her from a place of scarcity to one of abundance.

But what made Maya's success story truly inspiring and unexpected was her vulnerability. She shared her moments of doubt, her setbacks, and the times she questioned her ability to achieve financial freedom. In doing so, Maya created a safe space for others to embrace their own vulnerabilities and recognise that setbacks were simply steppingstones on the path to success.

As Maya continued, she highlighted the pivotal moment when she realised that her financial journey was not just about money but also about personal growth and self-discovery. She emphasised the power of mindset shifts, positive affirmations, and surrounding herself with a supportive community.

To everyone's surprise, Maya concluded her success story by inviting the audience to join her on a group challenge—30 days of financial mindset transformation. She handed out journals and encouraged everyone to write down their goals, affirmations, and daily reflections. Maya's infectious enthusiasm for personal growth and financial abundance ignited a fire within the audience, inspiring them to embark on their own transformative journeys.

In the weeks that followed, Maya's success story resonated deeply within the community. People started sharing their own financial challenges, triumphs, and newfound determination. They began to form accountability groups, meet regularly to discuss their progress, and cheer each other on. The Success Story Showcase became a catalyst for a supportive network of individuals committed to their financial well-being.

Maya's unexpected twist in her success story showcase revealed that true success lies not only in monetary achievements but also in the courage to share one's vulnerabilities and inspire others to embrace their own financial potential. Her journey became a shining example of the transformative power of perseverance, mindset shifts, and the unwavering belief that abundance is within reach for anyone willing to put in the effort.

From that day forward, Maya's success story continued to inspire generations to come. Her unexpected twist in the Success Story Showcase became a turning point for the community, igniting a ripple effect of personal growth, financial empowerment, and a collective belief that their dreams were indeed attainable.

Remember, it's often the unexpected and vulnerable moments within our success stories that leave the most profound impact on others. By sharing our journeys with authenticity and compassion, we inspire others to embrace their own paths to financial success, creating a community of unstoppable individuals ready to transform their lives and uplift those around them.

2. Financial Mentorship Program:

Become a financial mentor for someone who is seeking guidance and support on their own financial journey. This mentorship program allows you to share your knowledge, insights, and experiences with someone who can benefit from your wisdom. Schedule regular one-on-one meetings to discuss their goals, offer practical advice, and help them develop a personalised financial roadmap. Through your guidance and support, you'll inspire them to take control of their finances, make informed decisions, and create a future of abundance and fulfilment.

3. Empowering Financial Workshops:

Organise empowering financial workshops or webinars in your community or online. Use your expertise and passion to educate others on various financial topics, such as budgeting, investing, debt management, or building multiple streams of income. Create interactive activities, practical exercises, and engaging discussions that encourage participants to reflect on their own financial situations and take steps towards positive change. Through these workshops, you'll inspire and empower individuals to embrace their own financial power and cultivate a mindset of abundance.

Here is an example of an empowering financial workshop structure:

Welcome to the Empowering Financial Workshop, a transformative experience designed to equip you with the tools and knowledge to take control of your finances and create a future of abundance.

This workshop is structured to empower you to make informed financial decisions, cultivate a mindset of abundance, and embark on a journey of financial well-being. Here's an example of how the workshop could be structured:

1. Introduction and Icebreaker:

We begin by creating a warm and inclusive environment where participants introduce themselves and share one financial goal they aspire to achieve. This icebreaker activity fosters connection and sets the stage for a supportive and collaborative learning experience.

2. Understanding Your Financial Landscape:

In this session, we delve into the importance of understanding your current financial situation. We explore key concepts such as income, expenses, debt, savings, and investments. Through interactive exercises and discussions, you will gain clarity on your financial landscape and identify areas for improvement.

3. Building a Budget Blueprint:

Budgeting is a foundational tool for financial success. We guide you through the process of creating a personalised budget that aligns with your goals and values. You will learn practical strategies to track income, expenses, and savings, while also considering long-term financial objectives.

4. Exploring Multiple Streams of Income:

We expand our focus beyond traditional employment and explore the concept of creating multiple streams of income. Through case studies and group discussions, you will discover various avenues to generate additional income, such as side hustles, freelancing, or passive income sources. We'll help you identify opportunities that align with your skills, passions, and goals.

5. Investing for the Future:

Investing is a powerful wealth-building tool, but it can often feel overwhelming. In this session, we demystify the world of investing and provide you with practical guidance. You'll learn about different investment options, risk management, and strategies to grow your wealth over time. We emphasise the importance of starting early and provide resources to help you get started on your investment journey.

6. Protecting Your Financial Well-being:

Financial security goes beyond wealth accumulation. We discuss the importance of protecting your assets and mitigating risks through insurance, estate planning, and emergency funds. We provide insights and resources to help you make informed decisions in safeguarding your financial well-being.

7. Cultivating an Abundance Mindset:

To truly achieve financial success, we explore the power of mindset and its influence on our financial decisions. Through interactive exercises and guided reflections, we help you identify and transform limiting beliefs and negative associations surrounding money. You'll learn techniques to cultivate an abundance mindset, overcome scarcity thinking, and attract wealth through positive thoughts, intentions, and actions.

8. Action Planning and Commitment:

As we near the end of the workshop, we guide you in creating an action plan that consolidates your learnings and goals. You'll reflect on the key takeaways from each session and set actionable steps to implement your newfound knowledge in your financial journey. We encourage accountability partnerships within the workshop community to support each other on the path to financial success.

9. Closing and Celebration:

We conclude the workshop by celebrating your commitment to financial empowerment. Each participant shares one actionable step they plan to take immediately after the workshop. We foster a sense of community, inspiration, and ongoing support to ensure that your financial journey continues beyond this transformative experience.

Remember, this is just an example structure, the workshop can be tailored to meet the specific needs and interests of participants. The Empowering Financial Workshop is designed to provide you with the knowledge, skills, and support to embrace your financial potential and create a life of abundance

By engaging in these infectiously inspiring exercises, you'll unleash the transformative power of sharing your financial journey with others. Your stories, successes, and lessons will inspire individuals to believe in their own capabilities, break free from limiting beliefs, and pursue their own paths to wealth and fulfilment. Remember, your enthusiasm and willingness to help others on their financial journeys can create a ripple effect of positive change in their lives and beyond.

So, let your light shine bright and inspire others to embrace their financial potential. Share your stories, offer guidance, and celebrate the victories, no matter how big or small. Together, we can create a community of empowered individuals who believe in their ability to create a life of abundance, purpose, and fulfilment. Let the infectious inspiration begin!

CHAPTER 22
LEADING BY EXAMPLE

Becoming a beacon of financial enthusiasm and demonstrating how aligning passion, purpose, and prosperity can create a ripple effect of positive change.

Insight: Leading by Example is not about preaching or imposing beliefs onto others. It's about embodying your financial journey and authentically living a life aligned with passion, purpose, and prosperity. When you lead by example, you become a shining beacon of inspiration, illuminating the possibilities of financial abundance for others. Your actions, mindset, and enthusiasm for your own financial growth have the power to spark transformation in those around you.

Technique 1: Financial Enthusiasm Journal

Create a Financial Enthusiasm Journal to document and celebrate your own financial successes, breakthroughs, and lessons. Each day, take a moment to reflect on something positive or empowering that happened in your financial journey. Write it down, expressing your excitement, gratitude, and lessons learned. This practice not only reinforces your own mindset of abundance but also serves as a powerful reminder of the progress you've made. As you share your enthusiasm with others, you'll inspire them to embrace their own financial growth with optimism and excitement.

Here's an example of a page from a Financial Enthusiasm Journal:

Financial Enthusiasm Journal

Date: [Insert Date]

Today, I am overflowing with excitement and gratitude as I reflect on my financial journey. Every step forward brings me closer to a life of abundance, and I am eager to share my enthusiasm with the world. Here are the highlights from today's entry:

1. Celebrating a Financial Milestone:

I am thrilled to celebrate reaching a significant financial milestone. Through disciplined saving and smart investing, I have successfully achieved my savings goal for the year. This accomplishment fills me with immense pride and reinforces the power of consistent effort and financial focus. I am grateful for the progress I have made and excited about the possibilities that lie ahead.

2. Embracing a Growth Mindset:

Today, I had a breakthrough realisation about my mindset. I recognised that by shifting my perspective from scarcity to abundance, I open myself up to limitless opportunities. This mindset shift has allowed me to see the abundance that surrounds me and to attract even more prosperity into my life. I am inspired to continue nurturing this growth mindset and sharing its transformative power with others.

3. Paying It Forward:

In the spirit of financial enthusiasm, I performed a Random Act of Financial Kindness today. I anonymously donated to a local charity that supports financial literacy programs for underserved communities. It brings me great joy to contribute to a cause that aligns with my values and helps empower others on their financial journeys. The act of giving has reminded me of the abundance that flows when we share our blessings with others.

As I conclude today's entry, I feel an overwhelming sense of gratitude and excitement for the financial possibilities that lie ahead. My enthusiasm is infectious, and I can't wait to inspire others to embrace their own financial growth and create lives of abundance. Tomorrow is another day filled with opportunities, and I am ready to continue my journey with passion, purpose, and prosperity.

Remember, this example serves as a starting point, and you can customise your Financial Enthusiasm Journal to reflect your own experiences, achievements, and lessons. Let it be a space for celebrating your financial wins, expressing gratitude, and cultivating an unwavering enthusiasm for your financial journey.

Technique 2: Money Meetup Group

Organise a Money Meetup Group with like-minded individuals who are passionate about personal finance and financial growth. This group can meet regularly to discuss their financial goals, share success stories, exchange money-saving tips, and offer support and encouragement. Create a positive and uplifting environment where everyone feels comfortable sharing their financial journeys. By fostering a community of financial enthusiasm, you'll inspire and motivate each other to reach new levels of financial success. Consider incorporating fun activities such as financial challenges, guest speakers, or even financial-themed game nights to keep the enthusiasm flowing.

A short story to illustrate how a Money Meetup Group can unfold…

Once upon a time in a vibrant city, a group of enthusiastic individuals decided to form a Money Meetup Group. They were united by their shared passion for personal finance, their desire to grow their wealth, and their enthusiasm for supporting one another on their financial journeys.

The group consisted of people from different walks of life - young professionals, entrepreneurs, parents, and retirees - all with their unique financial goals and aspirations. They came together with open hearts and minds, ready to learn, share, and uplift one another.

At their first meetup, they gathered in a cosy cafe, buzzing with excitement and anticipation. The room was filled with laughter, as everyone introduced themselves and shared their financial aspirations. The atmosphere was warm and supportive, fostering a sense of camaraderie and connection.

During each meetup, the group engaged in various activities designed to enhance their financial knowledge and inspire them to take positive action. They exchanged money-saving tips, discussed investment strategies, and shared their success stories. They invited guest speakers from the financial industry, who imparted valuable insights and practical advice.

But the Money Meetup Group was not just about the technicalities of finance. They understood that true wealth encompassed more than just money. They explored topics such as mindful spending, aligning values with financial decisions, and the importance of giving back to their communities.

To keep the enthusiasm alive, they introduced fun activities and challenges. They organised "financial scavenger hunts" where participants had to find creative ways to save money or locate the best deals in the city. They held "financial-themed game nights" where they played interactive games that tested their knowledge and sparked lively conversations.

As the months went by, the Money Meetup Group became a tight-knit community. They celebrated each other's financial victories, no matter how big or small. They supported one another through setbacks and offered encouragement when challenges arose. The bonds they formed went beyond money; they became friends who genuinely cared for one another's well-being.

Outside of the meetups, they stayed connected through an online forum and social media. They shared articles, resources, and inspirational quotes that kept their financial enthusiasm ignited throughout the week. They cheered each other on as they achieved their goals and provided words of encouragement during times of uncertainty.

Through their Money Meetup Group, these individuals experienced a remarkable transformation in their financial lives. They learned from one another, gained new perspectives, and expanded their financial horizons. But perhaps most importantly, they discovered the immeasurable value of community and the power of supporting and inspiring others on their financial journeys.

Their Money Meetup Group became a shining example of how a shared passion for personal finance could create lasting connections and empower individuals to achieve their financial dreams. As they continued to gather, learn, and grow together, their enthusiasm spread like wildfire, inspiring many others in their community to start their own Money Meetup Groups.

And so, the Money Meetup Group's impact rippled far beyond their immediate circle, touching the lives of countless individuals who were inspired to take control of their finances, pursue their dreams, and create a future of financial abundance.

The End

Technique 3: Random Acts of Financial Kindness

Perform Random Acts of Financial Kindness to spread positive energy and generosity. Surprise someone with a thoughtful gesture related to their financial well-being, such as paying for a stranger's meal, offering to mentor someone in financial literacy, or gifting a book on personal finance to a friend. These acts of kindness not only brighten someone else's day but also demonstrate the power of aligning passion, purpose, and prosperity. By leading with generosity and kindness, you inspire others to embrace financial empowerment and share their own acts of financial kindness with the world.

Here's an example of the positive effect of receiving a random act of kindness:

Lucy had been feeling overwhelmed and stressed lately. Juggling work, family responsibilities, and financial pressures had taken a toll on her overall well-being. But one day, something unexpected happened that would change her perspective and brighten her day.

As Lucy walked into her favourite coffee shop, she noticed a vibrant poster on the wall. It read, "Random Acts of Kindness Day - Spread the Joy!" Intrigued, she approached the counter to learn more. The barista explained that they were celebrating the day by surprising their customers with random acts of kindness.

With a smile, the barista handed Lucy her usual coffee and said, "Today, your coffee is on us. Consider it a small token of appreciation for being such a wonderful customer." Lucy was taken aback by the gesture. She thanked the barista and couldn't help but feel a wave of warmth and gratitude wash over her.

As she sat down to enjoy her free coffee, Lucy's mood shifted. The weight of her worries seemed to momentarily lift, replaced by a sense of joy and optimism. It wasn't just the free coffee; it was the unexpected act of kindness that made all the difference.

That simple act of generosity brightened Lucy's day and ignited a renewed sense of hope within her. It reminded her of the goodness that exists in the world and the power of human connection. It was a gentle reminder that even amidst life's challenges, there were people who cared and were willing to extend a helping hand.

Buoyed by the positive energy, Lucy found herself paying it forward. She decided to perform her own random act of kindness by leaving a generous tip for the barista and writing a heartfelt note expressing her gratitude. She knew that by spreading kindness, she could make a positive impact on someone else's day, just as the barista had done for her.

The ripple effect of that simple act of kindness continued throughout the day. Lucy found herself smiling at strangers, holding doors open for others, and offering words of encouragement to those around her. She realised that even the smallest acts of kindness had the power to create a chain reaction of positivity.

That day, Lucy experienced first-hand the transformative power of receiving a random act of kindness. It reminded her of the beauty of humanity and the importance of spreading joy wherever she went. From that moment forward, she made a conscious effort to incorporate more kindness into her daily life, knowing that even the tiniest gestures could brighten someone's day and create a ripple of happiness in the world.

The positive effect of that random act of kindness stayed with Lucy, serving as a gentle reminder of the profound impact we can have on one another's lives. It inspired her to continue seeking opportunities to bring joy, kindness, and compassion to others, knowing that in doing so, she was contributing to a brighter and more compassionate world.

And so, that single act of kindness reverberated far beyond its initial encounter, touching not only Lucy's life but also the lives of those she encountered along her journey. It served as a powerful reminder that small acts of kindness have the potential to create a significant and lasting positive impact.

The End

Remember, leading by example is about sharing your financial journey, enthusiasm, and lessons learned with authenticity and compassion. By being a beacon of financial enthusiasm, you ignite a ripple effect of positive change, inspiring others to embrace their own financial growth and create a life of abundance. Let your passion, purpose, and prosperity shine brightly, lighting the way for others on their financial journey.

CHAPTER 24
SPREADING FINANCIAL LITERACY

Spreading Financial Literacy: Advocating for financial education and equipping others with the tools and knowledge to make informed financial decisions.

In a world where financial literacy is a superpower, the mission to spread financial education becomes a noble quest. Imagine a society where everyone possesses the knowledge and tools to make informed financial decisions, paving the way towards a brighter and more prosperous future. This is the vision that fuels the passion to advocate for financial literacy and empower individuals to take charge of their financial well-being.

Technique 1: Financial Escape Room

Step into the world of financial adventure with a thrilling and interactive experience known as the Financial Escape Room. This innovative technique combines the excitement of an escape room with the practicality of financial education. Participants are immersed in a scenario where they must solve financial puzzles, decipher clues, and make wise decisions to navigate their way out of the room. Through teamwork and critical thinking, they not only learn about various financial concepts but also develop problem-solving skills that can be applied in real-life situations. The Financial Escape Room creates an engaging and memorable learning experience that sparks curiosity and inspires a thirst for financial knowledge.

Here's a story about a thrilling financial escape room with some brilliant clues:

In the heart of the bustling city, a unique and mysterious establishment named "The Vault of Wealth" emerged. Rumours spread like wildfire about its hidden treasures and the enigmatic escape room it housed. This escape room, unlike any other, was designed to challenge participants' financial acumen and lead them to a great fortune.

As word of "The Vault of Wealth" spread, a group of adventurers, each with their own financial aspirations, gathered outside its imposing doors. The group consisted of Sarah, a young entrepreneur seeking financial independence; James, a seasoned investor yearning for his next big breakthrough; and Lily, a recent college graduate dreaming of a prosperous future.

As they entered the escape room, they were greeted by a peculiar host named Professor Prospero. With an air of mystery and excitement, Professor Prospero explained the rules of the game. Their mission was to solve a series of financial puzzles and unlock the vault within 60 minutes. Success would grant them not only a share of the treasure but also valuable financial knowledge.

The adventurers glanced around the room, their eyes drawn to an intricately designed wall adorned with various symbols and clues. The first clue, etched into an antique map, pointed them toward the concept of compound interest—the key to unlocking the first puzzle.

Their hearts raced as they deciphered the cryptic messages and solved the puzzles, each one unveiling a new clue and leading them closer to the treasure. They navigated through financial terms and concepts like budgeting, investing, and diversification, combining their knowledge and problem-solving skills to progress through the room.

As time ticked away, the adventurers encountered a particularly challenging puzzle, cantered around the concept of risk and reward. They had to carefully analyse financial scenarios and make calculated decisions to proceed. With determination and teamwork, they successfully cracked the code, propelling them further towards their goal.

The final puzzle stood before them—a labyrinthine maze representing financial independence. To escape the room and claim their reward, they had to demonstrate their understanding of personal finance and identify the steps necessary to achieve financial freedom.

With only seconds remaining, Sarah, James, and Lily pieced together the final clue. The walls of the escape room rumbled, and the vault door swung open, revealing a dazzling array of gold coins and jewels. Yet, the adventurers realised that the true treasure lay not in the material wealth before them but in the financial knowledge and wisdom they had acquired along their journey.

As they exited the escape room, their faces radiated with a newfound confidence. They had mastered the complexities of personal finance, transforming from adventurers seeking fortune to financial savvy individuals ready to conquer the world.

Inspired by their experience, Sarah, James, and Lily made a pact to share their newfound financial knowledge with others. They became advocates for financial literacy, organising events and workshops to educate their community. The escape room had not only brought them wealth but also sparked a desire to empower others on their financial journeys.

"The Vault of Wealth" became renowned as more than just an escape room—it became a symbol of financial enlightenment and transformation. People from all walks of life flocked to test their financial prowess and immerse themselves in the thrill of the puzzles. The escape room served as a beacon, inspiring individuals to unravel the mysteries of personal finance and embark on their own quests for financial success.

And so, the legend of "The Vault of Wealth" spread far and wide, leaving a trail of financially empowered individuals in its wake. The brilliant clues within its walls and the challenges they posed had forever changed the lives of those who dared to enter. The escape room had unlocked not only treasure but also a wealth of financial knowledge, transforming dreams into reality and empowering adventurers to create their own financial destinies.

The End

You may wonder what kind of clues there are:

Here are seven potential financial clues the adventurers encountered in "The Vault of Wealth" escape room, along with their corresponding answers:

1. Clue: "The power of compounding: Start with a penny, double it each day. In how many days will you have $1 million?"

Answer: 20 days

2. Clue: "Unlock the formula: Earnings before interest and taxes divided by total assets. What ratio are we referring to?"

Answer: Return on Assets (ROA) ratio

3. Clue: "Protect yourself: This three-digit number determines your creditworthiness. What is it?"

Answer: Credit Score

4. Clue: "Risk and reward: Which investment is considered the least risky?"

Answer: Government bonds

5. Clue: "Diversify for success: Spread your investments across different asset classes. What strategy are we referring to?"

Answer: Portfolio diversification

6. Clue: "Achieve financial freedom: This acronym stands for 'Financially Independent, Retire Early'. What is it?"

Answer: FIRE (Financial Independence, Retire Early)

7. Clue: "Securing your future: These retirement accounts offer tax advantages. Name one of them."

Answer: Individual Retirement Account (IRA)

Each clue presented a unique financial concept or term that the adventurers had to understand and apply to progress in the escape room. By solving these clues, they not only unravelled the mysteries of personal finance but also deepened their knowledge and awareness of various financial concepts.

These financial clues challenged the adventurers to think critically, apply their financial literacy, and make informed decisions, preparing them for future financial success beyond the confines of the escape room.

Technique 2: FinTech Game App

Embrace the power of technology and gamification with a FinTech Game App. This interactive mobile application combines educational content with a fun and immersive gaming experience. Players embark on a virtual financial journey, where they navigate financial challenges, make investment decisions, and manage their virtual finances. Through the game's engaging visuals, quizzes, and simulations, players gain practical insights into financial concepts and develop essential money management skills. The FinTech Game App appeals to individuals of all ages, making financial literacy accessible, enjoyable, and relevant in today's digital world.

Technique 3: Financial Storytelling Workshops

Unleash the power of storytelling to ignite financial curiosity and inspire action. Financial Storytelling Workshops bring together the art of storytelling and financial education, creating a captivating and transformative learning experience. Participants explore financial concepts and principles through thought-provoking stories that resonate on a deeper level. Facilitators use vivid narratives and relatable characters to convey complex financial topics in a simple and engaging manner. The workshops encourage participants to reflect on their own financial journeys, identify areas for improvement, and develop actionable strategies to achieve their financial goals. Financial Storytelling Workshops foster empathy, connection, and a sense of empowerment, equipping individuals with the knowledge and confidence to make informed financial decisions.

Here's an inspirational example of a financial storytelling workshop:

In a small community nestled by the river, a group of individuals gathered for a transformative experience—an immersive financial storytelling workshop. Each person brought their unique stories, hopes, and dreams, seeking guidance and inspiration to navigate their financial journeys.

The workshop began with a warm welcome from the facilitator, Sarah, a seasoned storyteller with a deep passion for financial empowerment. As the participants settled into the cosy room, Sarah invited them to embark on a journey of financial discovery through the power of storytelling.

Sarah wove captivating tales that illuminated the complexities of personal finance. She shared the story of Anna, a young artist who learned to navigate the ebb and flow of income while pursuing her creative passions. Anna's journey of financial resilience and resourcefulness resonated with the participants, sparking reflections on their own experiences.

As the workshop unfolded, Sarah encouraged the participants to share their own stories. They formed a circle of trust and vulnerability, where each person's narrative became a valuable lesson for the entire group. Emma, a single mother, shared her tale of overcoming financial challenges with determination and resilience, inspiring others to face their own obstacles head-on.

Throughout the workshop, the participants engaged in meaningful discussions, guided exercises, and reflective activities. Sarah skilfully wove financial concepts into the fabric of each story, making them relatable and accessible. They explored topics such as budgeting, investing, and financial goals, infused with the wisdom and insights gleaned from the stories shared.

One particularly poignant moment came when Mark, a retiree, recounted his journey from financial insecurity to financial freedom. His story painted a picture of hope and transformation, reminding everyone that it is never too late to take control of their financial futures. Mark's words stirred a fire within each participant, igniting a newfound determination to build a solid financial foundation.

The workshop concluded with a powerful exercise. Each participant crafted their own financial story, incorporating the lessons learned and their visions for the future. The room buzzed with creativity and excitement as stories were shared, amplified by a sense of unity and empowerment.

In the weeks that followed, the impact of the financial storytelling workshop rippled through the community. Participants, armed with newfound knowledge and inspired by the stories shared, began implementing practical financial strategies in their lives. Emma started a support group for single parents, sharing tips and resources for financial stability. Mark volunteered to teach financial literacy classes at the local community centre, empowering others with the tools to navigate their financial journeys.

The financial storytelling workshop had awakened a collective consciousness, transforming financial knowledge into action, and shaping a community built on financial resilience and empowerment. Each participant carried the stories and lessons with them, serving as beacons of inspiration for others seeking their own financial transformation.

The power of storytelling had illuminated the path to financial empowerment, bridging the gap between financial concepts and personal experiences. Through shared narratives, the workshop had fostered empathy, connection, and a sense of purpose. It had ignited a fire within each participant, fuelling their determination to shape their financial destinies and create a brighter future.

And so, the financial storytelling workshop became a catalyst for positive change—a ripple that extended far beyond its initial gathering. Through the magic of storytelling, the participants had discovered the power within themselves to shape their financial narratives, building a legacy of financial well-being and inspiring others to do the same.

The End

Through these exciting and innovative techniques, spreading financial literacy becomes an exhilarating adventure. By embracing the power of technology, storytelling, and immersive experiences, we can empower individuals to navigate the complex world of finance with confidence and competence. Together, let's advocate for financial education and equip others with the tools and knowledge they need to build a solid financial foundation and create a brighter future for themselves and their communities.

With these creative approaches, financial literacy becomes more than just numbers and concepts. It becomes an engaging and empowering journey of discovery, enabling individuals to take control of their financial destinies and create a ripple effect of positive change.

Together, let's embark on this mission to spread financial literacy, transforming lives and shaping a more financially empowered world.

CHAPTER 25
IGNITION...

In summary...

As we come to the close of our journey through "The Wealthy Soul: Ignite Your Passion, Work Less, Earn More," it's time to reflect on the transformative power of embracing your passions, finding purpose in your work, and cultivating abundance in all areas of your life. Throughout this extraordinary adventure, we have explored the depths of our souls, delved into the realms of possibility, and unlocked the secrets to living a truly fulfilled and abundant existence.

We have learned that true wealth goes beyond monetary gains and material possessions. It is the harmonious blend of passion, purpose, and prosperity that ignites our souls and propels us towards a life of profound fulfilment. By aligning our work with our deepest desires and values, we have discovered that the pursuit of success need not be a relentless struggle, but a joyful and meaningful journey.

In this pursuit, we have witnessed the incredible power of gratitude, compassion, and generosity. By nurturing authentic connections and contributing our unique gifts to the world, we have not only enriched the lives of others but also found immeasurable fulfilment within ourselves. We have learned that in spreading financial literacy and inspiring others with our stories, we create a ripple effect of positive change that transcends boundaries and empowers individuals to embark on their own paths to greatness.

Throughout this voyage, we have explored the intricate dance of time and tranquillity, understanding that by setting boundaries, practicing self-care, and finding balance, we create the space for our passions to thrive and our souls to flourish. We have harnessed the power of mindfulness and embraced the wisdom of flowing with the natural rhythms of life, allowing us to navigate challenges with grace and resilience.

As we conclude this chapter of our journey, let us carry the lessons and insights we have gained with us, allowing them to shape our lives and influence our choices. May we continue to nurture our passions, pursue our purpose with unwavering determination, and celebrate the abundance that flows into our lives. Let us be beacons of financial enthusiasm, inspiring others to embrace their own unique paths and experience the joy of aligning passion, purpose, and prosperity.

Remember, dear reader, that you possess within you the power to create the life you desire. It is the fusion of your dreams, talents, and unwavering belief in your own potential that will propel you towards extraordinary heights. So, go forth with confidence and a heart filled with gratitude, for the journey to wealth and fulfilment begins within you.

Embrace your passions, work with purpose, and watch as the universe conspires to bring forth abundance beyond your wildest dreams. May you ignite your soul, work less, and earn more in every sense of the word. The wealth of your soul awaits you.

With boundless gratitude and infinite possibilities,

The Wealthy Soul Seeker

Here is a call for you to take your steps to greatness…
Enjoy the journey…

In the realm where souls unite,
With hearts ablaze and spirits bright,
We gather here, a tribe of flame,
To ignite the world with our sacred name.

For we have journeyed, you and I,
Through depths of self, we dared to fly,
We've shed the doubts, the chains of old,
And found within, a story untold.

Now, hear the call, my fellow soul,
To venture forth and make life whole,
To share our gifts, our boundless light,
And raise the world to greater heights.

With hearts aglow and passion's fire,
We'll inspire others to aspire,
To tap into their wellspring deep,
And awaken dreams from dormant sleep.

For in our presence, they shall feel,
A higher vibration that can heal,
A resonance of truth and grace,
That lifts them to a higher place.

So let us walk, with purpose true,
In all we say and all we do,
To demonstrate our self-worth bold,
And show the world its own pure gold.

With every step, let kindness flow,
A beacon of love wherever we go,
Our actions speaking, without a word,

A testament to the greatness heard.

Together, we create a ripple vast,
A wave of change that's unsurpassed,
Encouraging others to take the leap,
To unlock their power, their dreams to keep.

For each soul touched by our light,
Will find their own path shining bright,
A symphony of souls, awakened, free,
Living in their worth and destiny.

So, my fellow journeyers, let us go,
Spread love and light, let the world know,
That wealth and abundance, in its core,
Is not just for some, but for all to explore.

Ignite the fire within your soul,
Inspire greatness, make others whole,
For in this dance of giving and receiving,
We find our purpose, a life worth living.

Embrace your gifts, let them unfurl,
And watch as transformation unfurls,
Together, we'll create a world anew,
Where greatness reigns, and love shines through.

R.A

www.ingramcontent.com/pod-product-compliance
Lightning Source LLC
Chambersburg PA
CBHW071052240526
45471CB00015B/1645